THE ENCHANTMENT OF GARDENS

A Psychological Approach

The Enchantment of Gardens

A Psychological Approach

Ruth Ammann

DAIMON
VERLAG

Title of the original German edition:
"Der Zauber des Gartens und was er unserer Seele schenkt"
Kösel Verlag, München, 1999

English translation by Mark Kyburz and John Peck

ISBN 978-3-85630-724-0
Copyright © 2008 Daimon Verlag, Einsiedeln

Cover photo: The Savill Garden near Windsor, England
(from the author's private archive)

Contents

Preface

First and foremost, I am indebted to all those magnificent gardens of my youth. They stirred my imagination from the outset and awakened innumerable memories and images in my soul that serve as my companions to this day. These images enter into my awareness only to vanish again behind the veil of the unconscious; they move, change, renew themselves, and enter into association with countless feelings in my heart. They are like a mountain of precious stones, including dark ones, among which I can play. Sometimes one stone lights up, sometimes another. I can only be deeply grateful for this treasure.

I also wish to thank all those individuals who have spent time with me in all those gardens I have visited and have taught me to feel my way into the profound soulfulness of gardens, and to understand and love it.

Furthermore, I express my gratitude to Aarau, the small town at the foot of the Jura hills where I was raised, and in particular its "Maienzug," an annual parade celebrating the beginning of summer (whose name derives not from the month of May but from the Swiss German word for a bunch of flowers). The town is adorned with flags, girls carry bouquets and wear fresh blooms in their hair, and men and boys wear flowers in their buttonholes. To this day, I associate the Maienzug parade with flowers, flags, a festive and joyous atmosphere, dancing and amorousness.

Since I was eager for my coronal and bouquet to sport the most beautiful flowers, I took up gardening as a girl and began growing my own flowers. Later, I wanted to become a gardener; my parents by no means forbade this, but they did urge me rather adamantly to graduate from high school first.

Their clear stance led me to engage with gardens in a different way at first: I studied architecture, a field in which gardens obviously play a role, if not a decisive one, as the outer space belonging to a house. Houses are a serious, solid, determined, and permanent affair! Yet gardens have always fascinated me on account of their vitality, versatility, unpredictability, and playful, even somewhat prankish nature. The world of gardens is very close to the feminine, owing both to its lively and playful attributes and its fecund, protective or aphrodisiac, Venusian qualities, such as beauty, joy, and sensuousness. These features struck a chord in me and enchant me to this day.

When I later began practising as a psychotherapist, I encountered the garden again as a soul garden that eludes us in general but which we can perceive with our mind's eye, and feel and experience within ourselves. Some people are able to use their hands to create and render visible or even tangible their inner images in various different ways, such as through painting or making clay figures, or creating images in a sandtray, a therapeutic method involving a small, sheltered "garden" that I often use in my practice. But no matter whether I am looking at the small soul garden that my patients have composed or if I am working with them in their inner garden, images of the outer garden serve me as companions time and again, lending me support and often consoling and regenerating me. Therapeutic work is difficult and often exhausting. The garden teaches me to have confidence in the healing power of the soul. Or as Kay Bradway, my dear friend, fellow Jungian analyst, and sandplay therapist, wrote in 1969: "While we can neither promise our patients a rose garden nor plant one for them, we can promise them a sheltered space in which they can let their own garden grow."

Over time, and owing to my various professional and private activities, my childhood notion that the garden of the soul and the soul of the garden are one and the same grew more and more certain. Garden and soul belong together; they form a mysterious space, between brightness and darkness, culture and nature, consciousness and the

unconscious, mind and body. The space in between has ensnared me and I set out to fathom it in this book.

In exploring my love of gardens, I also wish to seduce my readers to turn affectionately to their own souls, and to the spiritual world – the soul gardens – of others. I believe that our neglect of the world of the soul desolates our spiritual gardens and dramatically impoverishes humanity.

I have written this book with different people in mind. It is not intended to be a therapeutic book, although I will draw upon observations and experiences from my daily work in both my own soul garden and those of others. I also wish to weave what I experience in my own physical garden into this delicate fabric surrounding the subject of the "garden."

In the first instance, I hope to tempt my readers to open their "gates," for "the human senses are like the gates of a city: if the gates are open, there is life; if they are closed, it is desolate inside," as an Indian proverb phrases it. Let us thus walk across the Earth with open senses; our Earth is also a large garden requiring affection, devotion, and safeguarding. Only once we have recognized the goddess of love and life and accommodated her within ourselves will we be sufficiently steeled to face those forces in the world which are hostile to life. Put differently, only once the destructive forces of evil have frightened and shaken us enough will we be prepared to stoop to see and appreciate the beauty and vitality of the "small flowers" in the garden. That is, in both the outer and inner garden.

Chapter One

The Gate:
Entering into the Garden's Realm of Secrecy

My intense preoccupation with the "garden" began with a dream, like so much else in my life. I was returning from Brittany, that mysterious region where the spirits of nature take hold of human beings so that the spirit of nature can enter into magical association with the human soul. Where the old, sometimes hollow oak trees and the towering bracken, the dolms and menhirs, those mysterious recumbent and upright stones, the bubbling springs and pools, the old castle walls and derelict mills clad in ivy, all whisper: "Do you hear Merlin's voice? – Once you have heard it, you will never forget it." And: "Do you feel Vivian's veil enshroud you like wafts of glistening mist? Or are these moist cobwebs? But you will never again elude these delicate threads ... ."[1]

In any event, I must have fallen asleep traveling home from this world, which is so unlike the sterile and floodlit world of modern-day universities and offices. I dreamt of a clear, chartreuse forest. I was ascending a narrow path. The tracks of a cart were plainly visible. Where did they lead? Not far, I soon realized, as I suddenly stood before an enormous, massive wooden gate, which simply stood there with neither walls nor posts blocking my passage. Curiously, it was neither a common rectangular-shaped gate nor an arched Romanesque or Gothic gateway, but quite evidently an Oriental gate. It seemed to be firmly locked. Nevertheless, I tried to push it open; it opened, but only a fraction so that I could not see what lay behind.

– At this point I awoke. I was obviously confused upon awaking and a little sad, since who would not wish to know what new world lay beyond such a striking gate? In particular since I was able to open it just a fraction.

My companion said dryly: "Ah, now that is clearly the gate to the otherworld." Otherworld? Or another world? While this sounds so simple, it is not, for the otherworld is also known as the world of other being.[2] Other laws of time, space, and consciousness govern that world. I have read and heard a lot about this otherworld, perhaps even caught a glimpse or two of it, and – had I not just returned from an "otherworld" of sorts, one which covers Brittany like mist? Yet, had I really dreamed of the gate to the otherworld?

Gates and doors mark the transition from one space to another, such as from a street to a garden or from a garden to a house, to mention some of the most straightforward instances. Gates and doors safeguard the passage from the public to the private sphere, from the wild to a protected, cultivated area, or from a familiar interior to a perilous, hazardous exterior. Particularly ornate and important gates mark the transition from profane to sacred spaces, such as churches, temples, or sacred districts. There are, moreover, intangible gates, familiar from myths, dreams, and the imagination. We can perceive such gates and doors only with our mind's eye, hence making these part of each individual's spiritual wealth of images, so to speak. These can very well lead to the "other" world since they mark the transition from the individual spirit to the expansive soul of the world.

Since gates and doors enable the often difficult yet meaningful transitions from one world to another, from one mode of existence to another, they are surrounded by many rituals, which safeguard them and regulate human behavior in such places. Interestingly, there are in fact places where only a garden door marks the transition from the street to the garden, but no fence or hedge. The door alone suffices to denote the transition into another sphere.

The gate in my dream also stood alone in the boundless forest. There *had* to be something other beyond it than more forest. "My gate" was a particular beautiful and handcrafted specimen, which leads me to assume that it led to a garden also designed by humans.

Perhaps it was a lady forester's garden, since it lay in the forest? In that case, however, it must have been a "princely" one, since common forest witch's gardens have either small or scruffy or warped doors. Perhaps I assumed as much because it was an Oriental gate, or possibly a magic garden boasting a fountain at its center? – How ingenious our dreams are! Precisely because I could only open the door but a fraction, my curiosity would not loosen its grip.

Many years have passed since my dream during which I have explored many "worlds." I now know that the otherworld does not lie immediately behind the gate in my dream, but rather the twilight, in-between world of multiple inner and outer gardens. These are the small gardens between houses and streets, the gardens concealed between high walls, the bright and colorful gardens between farmhouses and fields, the stately and glorious gardens between castles and forests, the innumerable gardens between heaven and earth, nature and culture, between solid houses and animated, eventful, and wild surroundings. These gardens include the soul gardens between day and dream, the gardens connecting individuals or – even more beautifully – lovers, and the quiet gardens in which people discover the divine and thus themselves.

All these various gardens have preoccupied me, and I have explored them at home and abroad, among others in Oriental countries. Perhaps this explains why an Oriental arch embellished the gate in my dream, because it is precisely in Oriental culture or those under its influence where gardens are places in which external nature and the nature of the soul enter into the most enchanting association. And yet I have always returned to my bucolic Swiss garden that, as my daughter once said, I appear to love more than any other "possession." She is right. My garden is so dear to me because it is only one of my "possessions" and much rather part of who I am. In the garden, the outer world enters into association with the inner world to become that mysterious, animated twilight region where the tangible and intangible become one.

It seems to me that the "garden" is a highly complex symbol that affords us a particularly beautiful experience of the back and forth between the inner and outer worlds, and of their confluence; these movements are tangible and offer themselves to first-hand experience on the one hand, and have a spiritual-intellectual side on the other, resulting from the human experience of outer and inner gardens down the ages. Ultimately, I wish to convey my conviction that there is not merely an outer world which is divorced from the inner, but rather a world in-between in which both become superimposed and enter into association. In this world in-between, we spend time walking around and working in the garden with eyes looking at once outward and inward; we pick up floral scents and allow memories to rise within us; our hands touching the plants and soil evokes images in us of which we had no inkling beforehand. We then apprehend in a roundabout way, through our contact with flowers (as the German "durch die Blume" – literally, through the flower – phrases it more appositely), the greater scheme or feel embedded in the large context of meaning formed by nature.

Each individual's subjective relationship to the garden, to the world in-between, strikes me as most important. Hence, this book offers neither an exclusively historical account of gardens and the nature of plants, nor a chart of the meaning of gardens in dreams, fairy tales, and inner images; rather I wish to express my personal feelings for gardens, since this book arises primarily from my *love* of and affection for gardens. My desire to experience this love and shape it into a book originated not from an image but from a fragrance.

I was sitting on the terrace of a small Irish country house, not on its glorious side facing the large lawn and sea, but on the side where there was a small, concealed, old-fashioned garden. At that moment,

a gentle breeze swept the smell of old roses from the garden to where I was sitting – and transported me back playfully to the gardens of my childhood. (I had had the good fortune of being allowed to roam around and discover several splendid old gardens as a child.) I knew which rose emitted this scent, and I got up to find it in this secluded Irish garden. As I walked up and down the gravelled paths between the rose beds, which were exactly akin to the boxed flower beds of my youth, I discovered that very same rose, bearing white petals touched with pink, together with many, many memories of my garden adventures as a child. My mind's eye conjured up my grandfather's carnations, my grandmother's roses, our version of hide-and-seek in that almost labyrinthine flower garden, the pile of beans await-

ing busy hands, as well as the potatoes and cockchafer grubs on our playing field during the "scramble to grow crops" dur-ing World War Two.[3] All these events seemed minor and neg-ligible, but they proved highly significant for my later life, and so I wish to link them to ob-servations during the course of this book. Recollecting the various strands of my life af-fords me the opportunity to make out a part of the pattern in the carpet that my fate is weaving.

For now, let us leap from the gate appearing in my dream on my way home from Brittany to a specific and tangible gate. It is spring-time. Still utterly overwhelmed by the architectural beauty of the shaded interior of the Alcazar palace in Seville in southern Spain, my eye suddenly drifts through the high, ornate arched windows out into the green exterior to catch sight of a play of light and shade. The wonderful fragrance of wisteria, orange blossoms, roses, and other

flowers eluding my eye draws me outside. I delve into the garden through a gate.

Many people are strolling along the paths, admiring the orange trees bearing both blossoms and fruits, listening to the birds, and enjoying the sight of the white pigeons fluttering to and fro between the palm tree tops and the purling fountain. The pigeons perch themselves on the fountain edge or on the head of the bronze figure from where they observe the visitors in the garden. The visitors are peaceful, strolling slowly and enjoying the colors and shapes of the plants, the fragrant blossoms, and the birdsong. They touch the leaves and flowers and smile. Oddly enough, even tall and able-bodied mean and strapping youths have a peaceful air about them, quite unlike on the city streets. It seems as if a spell has been cast over those visiting the garden: while their eyes seem to be looking outward, beholding the beauty of the garden, they are also cast inward – but where to? Many appear to be dreaming with open eyes – but what about?

Perhaps the magic of the outer garden leads them to another world, to the inner garden, the garden of their souls. What they see there escapes us. Only the expression on their faces tells us that it must be a world of peace and joy, or they would hardly look so relaxed and happy. Could it be that their slow and leisurely promenading affords them time affectionately to feel their way into this setting? Could it be that as they turn unbiased toward the beauty and sensuousness of the palace gardens, they are guided toward inner beauty and joy, peace and gratitude? Could it be that a gardener's affectionate devotion communicates itself to the garden's visitors? Could it be that

the garden leads, or even seduces, us softly and playfully to those feminine values that we suppress in everyday life, or even loathe or consider superfluous?

I do not know for sure. Observing people strolling in gardens over many years gives me reason to believe that gardens have a particular effect on us. Many people fall silent, and move almost meditatively from one plant to the next. Inner images, memories, and many different feelings are bound to arise within them. They allow themselves to be stirred by the secret of life and growth, becoming and decay, the visible and invisible, the subsoil and the subterranean. Others give loud expression to their surprise and delight at discovering something beautiful or moving. They can be heard chattering and laughing. Children also laugh and cry out, jump around and play. They are akin to flowers, for these also play. Like children, flowers neither work nor sleep but instead dance in the wind in a play of colors and shapes.

Gardens playfully evoke feelings, images, fantasies that lead us to the world of the imagination in which the psychic and physical-material are no longer separate. This in-between world of the imagination is something quite particular, constituting a talent unique to human beings.[4] It plays its game in many places, in particular in the outer garden and the soul garden – both are worlds that humankind has nurtured for millennia and interwoven in the most beautiful fashion time and again.

Many threads and many weavers engage in weaving the magic carpet of a garden: nature, the great weaver, has a nurturing and creative effect, not only through her plants that grow and wither in the short rhythm of night and day as well as larger seasonal change. The countless animals, including worms and mice in the soil, chafers, beetles, birds, butterflies, and many others are at work uninterrupted. And just as many people are involved in the weaving. They imagine, plan, love, and curse the garden. Whereas many threads of sweat, chagrin, vexation, joy, desire, and surprise are all woven in the garden carpet, purposeful aggression is less frequent (at best affecting unimaginative and insensitive gardeners, since gardens do not incite aggression). Gardens, however, try human patience: both outer and inner gardens develop slowly and require much time.

But one side of nature also prevents the weaving from reaching an end, for it never ceases transforming or destroying what has been created, changes colors, and induces plants to wither and die. Human beings, too, wreak destruction because there is good reason to or because their patience snaps or because they are dissatisfied. Thus, all is subject to a constant interplay of growth and decay, becoming and dissolution, human toil and pleasurable rest. Whether or not we are aware of it, a wisdom and force that is nothing less than divine is pervasive.

Does the nature of the garden not recall the nature of the soul? Since I believe that it does, and because they have much in common, I hence endeavour to weave the fantasies, thoughts, dreams, and experiences of my patients, friends, and myself into a book about "the soul of the garden and the garden of the soul." In what follows, the reader should not be alarmed by my moving back and forth between the inner and outer world, fantasies, dreams, and real events. I am simply busy weaving a small part of the great garden carpet.

If we conjure up a garden carpet in our mind's eye, this image recalls those magnificent old Persian carpets that P.R.J. Ford refers to as "knotted gardens" in his marvelous *Oriental Carpet Design*. These carpets are artistic manifestations of nomadic dreams. Ford reminds

us of Iran's neverending greyish brown desert, whose sand consists of dust, rocks, and stone, and suggests that it is hardly coincidental that the most splendid "gardens" could actually be found depicted in the carpets lying on the floors of the desert peoples' houses. Following age-old customs, the patterns of the carpets were modeled on the singular design of Persian gardens.

Ford observes: "What is probably the most famous carpet in history had such a design. It was produced [...] for the palace at Ctesiphon of Chosroes (Khosroes) I, one of the last Persian emperors before the Arab conquests of the seventh century AD. It is reported to have been some 27 m (90 ft) wide and five times as long, and its fabric was embellished with silk and thousands of pearls and jewels."[5] And, as Marie-Luise Gothein notes in her two-volume history of gardening: "The carpet background depicts the pleasure garden, through which rivers and paths run back and forth transversally, and which is lavishly embellished by trees and charming spring flowers. Its broad, encompassing border features flower beds planted with an array of differently colored blossoms, represented by blue, red, yellow, white, and green stones. On the background, gold imitates the yellowish soil, stripes symbolize the river banks, and crystal clear stones deceptively represent the waters in-between. Small, pearl-size stones intimate the gravel paths. Stems and branches were made of gold and silver, the foliage was woven from silk, and the fruits were crafted from colorful rock."[6]

This is the oldest account of the carpet known as King Chosroes's spring garden. He had the carpet displayed in winter to "remind him of spring." The Arab conquerors subsequently tore the carpet asunder. Numerous attempts were made to recreate the pattern of Chosroes's legendary spring garden, but alas these were all in vain.

If I project myself into the soul of a person exhibiting a garden carpet in winter so as to "recall spring," I imagine the carpet bearing aloft that individual through a cold, bleak, and austere winter like a vision of returning life, beauty, warmth, sensuality, and fertility. From everyday experience and psychotherapeutic practice, we are familiar with the "spiritual winter" during which the world and life appear dark, cold, and dead, or those "spiritual deserts" in which inanimateness, aridity, and neverending monotony govern the human soul. Should these desert moods afflict our fellows or patients for long, that is, if the spiritual winter never seems to end, this proves difficult for all concerned and may be contagious. Like Chosroes, the Persian king, we then need the vision of a garden in bloom, one that carries us through winter.

Some readers might consider the vision of a blooming garden paradisal and thus "aloof" and unrealistic. It seems to me that only those who have never woven a carpet or grown a blooming garden might see matters this way. Both activities call for such a lot of concrete work, love, and patience that achieving even the most simple, animated soulic garden would be impossible without some vision of a blooming paradisal garden. We will encounter this kind of work in the soul garden later on.

Chapter Two

The Meaning of Fences: What Makes a Piece of Earth into a Garden?

Before examining the nature and secrets of various kinds of gardens more closely, I wish to consider the meaning of the word "garden." In Middle High German, a garden was a "garte" (as in contemporary Swiss German), and "garto" in Old High German. In Gothic, "garda" denotes a cattle hurdle, and "gards" signifies a homestead, house, and family. In English, the word "yard" refers to a farmyard, while the Swedish "gard" means a homestead, grange, estate, plot. These terms derive from the Indo-Germanic word "ghordo," that is, wickerwork, fence, enclosure, stockade, hence denoting a fenced-in or enclosed area or plot of land in the broadest sense. These terms are akin to "choros," an open-air dance floor, and the Latin "hortus" for garden. Originally, the Russian word "gorod" (a town or city) also denoted "an enclosed place."

Incidentally, "paradise" has the same meaning, originating from the Old Iranian words "pairi" (enclose, surround) and "daeza" (wall). Thus, paradise is first of all a place or site surrounded by a wall. However, it encloses a particularly sacred place, namely the Garden of Eden, the garden of bliss.

In order to delimit the term "garden" clearly from "house," we must consider the origin of the latter. "House" is akin to "skin" and derives from "cover" or "encase." A house is thus a completely encased space, covered on all sides, top, and bottom. It is man-made and reiterates the enclosure, encasement, seclusion, or sequestering of a clearly

designated area or space that serves as living quarters for an individual or group. Like a settlement or town, houses are creations of human architecture or culture in a broader sense. Thus, they contrast inherently with nature – a completely enclosed interior affording its inhabitants protection and identity on the one hand, and the open expanse of an undesigned and unsecured exterior on the other.

In contrast, a garden is a fenced-in plot of ground, enclosed and bounded on a horizontal but not on a vertical plane. It can also be a piece of nature that has been brought inside, either domesticated or transformed and cultivated, such as those splendid quadrangles, interior yards, and garden courtyards familiar from Islamic architecture. These, too, are open toward the sky, that is, natural light, sun, and rain. As we will see, precisely this bounding on the horizontal, mundane, human level, but not on the vertical one connecting heaven and earth, defines the specific nature of the garden. For now, let us remain on terra firma, on the horizontal plane. In the first instance, a "garden" is thus a plot of ground delimited and enclosed from boundless nature.

Human beings have always attached utmost significance to owning a demarcated plot of ground, that is, a contained, overseeable, protected area or space. Its boundaries frame an individual's life and existence, or that of a family or specific group. Within these boundaries or confines, human beings can create their own world and establish their own personal order. The boundless wilderness spells chaos for them, evoking a sense of forlornness and anxiety.

We are currently experiencing the opposite today, namely that many people feel constrained by their protected, bounded garden. Their personal, ordered world has grown too familiar and bores them, and they hence seek the vastness and "disorderliness" of the wilderness again. They are drawn to outdoor adventure in unspoiled nature (or "free" nature, as German phrases it) in their quest to experience what looks outwardly new, but also perhaps to behold new inner images and visions. Basically, however, human beings fear the foreign, chaotic, and disorderly in every respect – in concrete physical terms as well as inwardly and spiritually. They only feel at home once they have established their own confined, overseeable world, which they can negotiate on their own terms.

Thus, we first establish boundaries or erect a fence or enclosure to delimit our plot of ground from the entirely Other, that is, boundless nature (also known as the wilderness) as well as from plots belonging to others. But what makes us draw a boundary? Why do we demarcate ourselves from others and, by implication, exclude or even segregate the Other? (Has this ever occurred to you? Perhaps it did the last time you were painting your garden fence and felt exasperated by the neverending slats standing sentinel over the boundaries of your plot of ground like soldiers on ramparts? Or you might have done so when you marveled at your neighbor's towering shinglewood hedge, which obscures even a giant's view across?) But I obviously have in mind not merely those boundaries that individuals or families draw around their plot of ground, but also the municipal boundaries (walls used to mark the limits of a village or town) and national borders erected by groups and peoples.

Enclosing or fencing in a plot of land affords protection against intruders or indeed the foreign. It also constitutes an act of self-manifestation in that we declare: "I live here, this is my 'kingdom,' and the law and order established here are mine." We thus dissociate ourselves as individuals or as cohesive group from either the larger human collective or vast, unknown nature. Presumably you will have pondered these matters yourself or experienced them in one way or another. Fences, or similar forms of enclosure, also imply our desire to live peacefully within our boundaries. The German word for cemetery – "Friedhof" – consists of "Friede" (peace) and "Hof" (yard); a cemetery is thus a garden that we protect and encircle with a wall to afford the souls of our deceased rest and peace. Neither hatred nor claims to power, neither noise nor commotion, nor similar stealthy enemies of human peace, are meant to invade this final resting place, this garden of souls.

Gardens are encircled with fences or walls above all to protect them against undesired intruders, such as animals, and against devastation and misappropriation. They serve to protect the right to privacy as well as human habitats comprising dwellings and a garden, that is, a plot of usable ground. The invulnerability of boundaries has always formed an essential basis for collective life, and enjoyed utmost protection, including legal protection. Trespassing upon or unlawfully entering privately owned land remains liable to prosecution to this day.

As proprietors, we preside over our premises and garden as lords and masters. We thus exercise power over our garden and can within reason do with it as we please: we can either love, cultivate, and grow it or neglect it and let it grow wild. We cover it with concrete slabs, thus depriving it of soil and fertility, its foundations. Or we choose to subjugate it completely, transforming it into a violated piece of earth no longer recognizable as a garden.

Notwithstanding dissociation and enclosure, we should not forget that not only human activity brings life to the garden but so do plants and animals. Gardens, moreover, are unbounded toward the sky and the depths of the earth. No boundaries exist in either case. If we aspire to live in peace and harmony with our garden, we must negotiate an egalitarian partnership not only with plant and animal life but also with various natural elements, such as heat, drought, storms, rain, hail, and frost. The garden thus curtails human self-importance. Fences therefore both delimit human delusions of grandeur and protect the space in which we can learn to encounter nature with modesty and humility.

"Independence is a political, not a scientific, term," Lynn Margulis notes in her book, *What is Life?* In the same passage, she writes: "The autopoietic view of life differs from standard teachings in biology. Most writers of biology texts imply that an organism exists apart from its environment, and that the environment is mostly a static, unliving backdrop. Organic beings and environment, however, interweave. Soil, for example, is not unalive. It is a mixture of broken rock, pollen, fungal filaments, ciliate cysts, bacterial spores, nematodes, and other microscopic animals and their parts. 'Nature,' Aristotle observed, 'proceeds little by little from things lifeless to animal life in such a way that it is impossible to determine the exact line of demarcation.'"[7]

Thus, any haughtiness or arrogance toward nature, be it "merely" toward the earth or plant and animal life, is inappropriate. Life is sacred wherever it occurs and takes effect. This knowledge is firmly anchored in good and loving gardeners, whose work rests upon it as a cornerstone.

Fences therefore have various functions. They obviously protect our plot and property against trespassers and other forms of outside encroachment. After all, they safeguard both what has great value, namely the food and sustenance often grown in gardens, and the flowers and trees affording us pleasure. Not least they guard our homes, which we instinctively defend as our own "skin." Fences as such touch upon fundamental, material, existential, and emotional values. Fences or enclosures in general also serve to protect what is effectively a most intimate sphere, in which we can learn and live modesty and respect for nature and divine creative power. The horizontal, earthly boundary thus protects our relationship with the cosmos as well as that between humankind, nature, and God. We speak far less often about this deeper meaning of the garden fence.

Fences thus safeguard that sphere in which the human soul can encounter and coalesce with the soul of the garden. This connection with the completely Other affords us a profound experience of the divine, which thereby strikes root in our soul. The outer garden receives an inner counterpart – the psychic or spiritual garden. The latter constitutes a sacred space because it no longer merely serves material "possession" but also inner "being."

In symbolic terms, fences or walls turn a plot of ground into an enclosure akin to the hermetic vessel employed in alchemical operations to cook, process, and transform raw source material into a precious material ("gold"). In their endeavor to completely refine the outer material, alchemists simultaneously sought to ennoble and foster inner, intellectual-spiritual values. In what was a holistic process, they linked outer, concrete work with gaining inner knowledge and personal growth. True gardeners do likewise, for they are alchemists in a garden receptacle.[8] Like the alchemists' work, that of gardeners also moves back and forth between the outer, tangible world and the inner, spiritual world. Based on my experience with gardeners or "garden people," outer, physical activity, that is, being and meditating in a garden, also animates and develops spiritual life; and vice versa, work in the inner garden also affects outer life, as we will see in the last chapter. To my mind, there is no purely outer or inner garden; rather, the garden is forever a world in-between.

But let us turn to real gardens and how our ancestors (and spiritual forebears) took possession of their plots. Evidently, they did not consider land either as an inanimate object or an object of financial speculation in modern parlance, nor did they consider the enclosure or fence erected around it merely as dead wood. Countless rituals for the safeguarding of border fences were performed, for nature was said to be animate, and there was an ever-present danger that evil spirits, demons, witches (or so-called "fence riders"), [9] illnesses, and other untoward phenomena would intrude into the garden. Such threats had to be deterred through magic procedures in order to preserve peace on the inner side of the fence.

Here I wish to weave a small episode from contemporary everyday life into the fabric of this chapter to indicate just how current such rituals are today:

Two little girls, one aged nearly three with a blond ponytail and the other aged four with brown curly hair, are sitting in a garden near the fence. Through the fence they can see down into a small gorge through which a little stream flows and the nearby dark forest. Suddenly they come running into the house: "A wolf! A wolf! There's a wolf in the forest!"

The grandmother wants to calm the girls and accompanies them into the garden. "So where's this wolf? I can't see one?" "There! Over there! In the forest!," the girls scream. "I see," the grandmother says, "but there's a fence between the forest and you. And our dog is in the house; he'll protect you." The girls yield. Soon afterwards, the grandmother sees them sitting in exactly the same spot near the fence and hears them chatting away keenly. She approaches them softly and listens. She hears them assuring each other in great earnest that while the evil wolf is in the forest, the forest lies on the other side of the fence. There was another wolf, a dog, on this side of the fence, in the garden. But this wolf is good. They were safe because the good wolf was protecting them against the evil wolf.

At bedtime the little blond girl says to the grandmother: "Our dog is good and will protect me against the evil wolf, won't he? And the evil wolf is outside the fence, isn't he? She then counted a number of other angels watching over her sleep, but the good dog and the fence were the two most important ones.

*

Obviously, the episode had great importance for the girls. It would have been pointless to reason them out of the fact that there was a dark, evil wolf, for even small children know that good and evil exist in life. On the one hand, they know that the wolf embodies evil from Grimm's fairytales.[10] For example, "The Wolf and the Seven Young Kids" contrasts the wolf, as the embodiment of evil and darkness, with the white, benign (and somewhat too trusting!) goats. "Little Red Riding Hood" establishes the wolf as decidedly evil, deceitful, and devouring. On the other hand, children already have a sense of the dark and frightening from an early age. How else could we explain that they suddenly cry out "I am afraid!" for no apparent reason. Fear descends upon them like a dark cloud only to pass quickly in most cases. Much earlier in life, prior to speech, a shadow or frown sometimes crosses their little faces, like a sign of an inner foreboding of dark forces.

Hence we cannot make our children believe that there are no evil and dark forces. But if they learn to recognize the family dog as the evil wolf's good counterpart, and that the garden fence stands pro-

33

tectively between the familiar garden and the unknown, fear-inspiring forest, this soothes their young souls and lets them sleep in peace. The magic procedure which protected the girls against evil (garden gnomes are said to have this power, too ...) consisted of repeating the words that the evil wolf was really outside the fence and that the family dog was indeed protecting them.

Let us return to the rituals that our ancestors performed to protect their gardens and their outer boundaries: the garden or the plot of ground had to be free of negative forces, precisely because they were sacred places, dissociated from profane chaos. Hence, ancient land-taking rituals and demarcations were sacred enactments. They were performed ceremoniously, placing the garden or the enclosed plot of ground under the protection and mercy of a godhead that represented much greater power than that available to any individual. And among certain peoples they go on being performed to this day. Often, altars were erected, and a boundary sacrifice was made.[11] These ritual performances manifested the fact that the earth belongs not to man but to God; neither do we have absolute ownership over our gardens, but they constitute at most what we may attend to and nurture. They are the plots of ground delighting us and over which we grieve, and whose prospering ultimately lies beyond our power.

Precious little has survived of this stance. Today, instead, we presume that the earth is ours. Often, we attempt to rule the outer garden, our own inner garden, and the psychic or spiritual garden of others. Alas, "gardens" are afflicted with much unkindness and improvidence. Notwithstanding uncharitableness and a craving for power, I would argue that entering a plot of ground one has just purchased or is about to purchase remains a numinous experience. Knowing that "this plot is mine, and this is where I can build a house and plant a garden" evokes a profound and primordial sense of happiness in most people.

Likewise, children are happy and proud to be assigned their own patch in their parents' garden. Symbolically, they experience exactly the same sense of creating a world as adults do when digging, planting, and arranging a garden. Creatively shaping one's own habitat will probably remain numinous forever, for this is an instance in which a small spark of the great creation lights up.

In this respect, I recall a friend's magnificent garden, hardly larger than an average-size parlor, amid a sprawling modern city. She showed me pictures of this small plot of ground when she took it over: they feature a wall and a some kind of lattice encompassing a patch of soil, some stone slabs, and some neglected plants. Only the boundary suggested that a garden actually existed here (see illustrations on following page).

Today, however, my friend's garden is a small Garden of Eden: ivy, roses, and clematis climb the walls and lattices. Bushes and their many-shaped leaves and shades of green form the backdrop for the radiant colors of all kinds of flowers abloom all year. Nor should I forget to mention the birds whose song resounds through the garden and who drink from the small, romantic fountain. My friend either works in the garden or dwells at leisure on a small bench. Both activities afford her the peace, joy, and regeneration of vigor that she needs for her professional work and to cope with hectic city life. Her little garden also includes the "vertical" axis mentioned above: a short distance beyond the garden wall a church spire soars heavenward, while the earth in which her flowers root downward she attends to, waters, and nurtures. She has managed with much love to create her own small and very personal world in close communion with nature.

There are medieval depictions of small gardens that look like a wickerbasket filled with flowers. Basketweaving follows the same principles as wattled fences. Thus, I liken my friend's little garden to a basket full of flowers amid the concrete urban jungle.

I conclude this chapter with a small series of dreams from a twelve-year old boy (let us call him "Peter") to reveal which significance a garden and a garden fence in particular could have for a young person's spiritual development.

He dreamt that there were other rooms in his parents' house that he had not yet discovered. In his dream, the house appeared as he had known it for twelve years. – Some months later he dreamt that he built his own house on the meadow behind his parents' house, but that the two buildings were connected by a bridge. – A few months after that, he dreamt that the bridge between the two houses had disappeared and that the plot of land on which his house stood was now enclosed by a sturdy fence. His house now stood within the enclosure, surrounded by a splendid garden full of plants and animals.

*

I will discuss the first two dreams only briefly in order to focus on the motif of the garden and fence in particular.[12]

Evidently, Peter's all too familiar parental home has become too confining, and he now seeks new scope and opportunities for development. A dream comes to his aid and declares: "There is new space, but you have yet to discover it." The adumbration or discovery of hitherto unknown space is a rather frequent dream motif. It is linked to those forbidden rooms in fairy tales to which we are denied access, but are bound to enter. Forbidden rooms *must* be entered and unknown spaces *must* be sought, for new life seeks to manifest itself in forbidden or unknown, *empty* spaces, precisely the life that *must* first find space within the fairy-tale hero or dreamer to be recognized and lived.

Peter's second dream reveals what he discovers in the unknown rooms. The vision features Peter's parental home, his own house, and a bridge in between. The two houses are connected like one body to another. Is this the image of the umbilical cord connecting a mother and her new-born infant? That is, an image of natural birth? No, this is another kind of birth, since Peter says that in his dream he has built his house himself. This is rather the image of actively leaving his parents' spiritual house to enter his own. It denotes the beginning of a transition into a life for which he will now assume responsibility.

In Peter's third dream, the bridge connecting his own house with his parents' has gone. Instead, he has erected a fence around his garden to mark off his own plot of ground from that of others. Peter's unconscious indicates his development toward independence already at an early stage of his life. His dream actually asserts: "Please leave me be and respect who I am." Yet what does he feel compelled to defend himself against? External aggressors or wild animals? Certainly not, but possibly against thoughtless, perhaps even well meant incursions of family members or friends.

Adults often have little consideration for their children's soul gardens; it could be argued that they actually fail to perceive their children's spiritual world, presumably as little as their own! Yet all kinds of feelings about life start growing in a child's "garden" from an early age, comparable to those plants growing in a real garden: small, timid wallflowers; trusting, blue-eyed forget-me-nots; proud, beaming sunflowers; delicate violets; and wonderfully fragrant roses protecting themselves with their thorns. Considering that so many feelings and emotions grow in the soul garden, is Peter not right to build a protective fence around his house? In particular at his age, at the onset of puberty, the most vulnerable flowers, namely feelings for the opposite sex, begin to grow in the human soul. These are the most timid and personal that a young person can experience, and must under no circumstances be trampled upon with indiscreet questions or mockery. Besides, it is crucial for young individuals to draw a clear and firm boundary between their psychological personality and the outside world and the Other, all the more because external notions often besiege them, and their own dreams and fantasies like to explode the limits of what is possible.

Yet adults also experience difficulties with their boundaries in that "weeds" grow under or over the fence. It seems to me that it is only with age that the quality of the "plants" growing in the soul garden gains the upper hand over sheer quantity. Inner growth is no longer quite as rampant and boundless, and slows down on the horizontal plane. Instead, soul plants now grow downward rather than upward

toward the sky. The fence is no longer required as much as previously, and may now grow old and somewhat warped, just as an elderly person's arms no longer need to embrace so much outer life.

Perhaps the elderly experience what Carl Gustav Jung writes at the very end of his memoirs: "This is old age, and a limitation. Yet there is so much that fills me: plants, animals, clouds, day and night, and the eternal in man. The more uncertain I have felt about myself, the more there has grown up in me a feeling of kinship with all things. In fact it seems to me as if that alienation which so long separated me from the world has become transferred into my own inner world, and has revealed to me an unexpected unfamiliarity with myself."[13]

Chapter Three

The Soul's Half-Acre:
From Outer to Inner Garden

In attempting to explore the inner spiritual sphere or what I call the soul garden more closely, I return to some aspects of the outer garden. Gardens are mostly planted in close proximity with the house(s) to which they belong. Sometimes they lie between a house and free, unspoiled nature; in urban environments, they more often occupy a space between the principal house and other gardens, houses, and streets. On the one hand, the garden constitutes what lies between the known and unknown, between human edifices and natural growth; on the other, it occupies an interstice in which various opposites – culture and nature, the built and natural – enter into association.

Gardens would not exist without either human constructive consciousness or the existence of nature, plants, and animals. They are the new factor. Or in different terms, they are the child loved by all, arising from the marriage of nature and culture – the child with a thousand faces, shamelessly revealing its diversity and yet never disclosing its secrets. Gardens are akin to us, for we also invest a lot of who we are in them. And yet they surprise us and seem strange, for their naturalness represents the completely Other that we can only wonderingly accept but never actually comprehend.

Whether on its tangible surface or in inner, symbolic terms, this "garden-child" forever constitutes some kind of world in-between. A scale model of Cluny, a charming medieval town in east-central

France, beautifully illustrates the gardens occupying the space between the townhouses lining the streets and the large, contiguous fields lying beyond the gardens.[14] Medieval towns in Switzerland and elsewhere in Europe were conceived in the same manner: the townhouses are entered directly from the lanes, while the long gardens behind the houses extend either toward open fields or other gardens, houses, and lanes.

In the modern districts of such towns one first enters a small front garden that forms a space between street and house. Here the visitor catches an initial glimpse of the residents' "face," perhaps not in all its intimacy but as a first amiable welcoming smile. Considering that front gardens and entrances often have an impersonal and stiff air about them, this smile is possibly simply a representative mask donned for the visitor's sake: "After all, one does not wear one's heart on one's sleeve."

Yet such a dismissive attitude is not the rule. For example, London's long rows of Victorian townhouses boast very appealing, mostly lovingly cared for front gardens. Together with the front entrances,

all shaped the same way and yet sporting different colors, these gardens already offer a certain insight into the character of their residents. These are friendly garden spaces, inviting us to an initial encounter. Only later, when visitors have become friends, are we led through the house to the garden concealed at the back.

By contrast, the stately gardens of castles and other aristocratic homes mostly stretch out between the buildings and a forest belonging to

the grounds. Such gardens occupy a space between the house, which bears witness to a specific cultural era, and unspoiled nature. They are examples of well arranged, domesticated nature. For example, the Château de Vaux le Vicomte[15] is not an intimate, private habitat but the collective expression of a grandiloquent attitude prevalent at the time. The garden plants have been straitjacketed into architectonic forms that echo and extend the castle's architecture. Such gardens afford nature little life of its own but completely subordinate it to an era's sense of aesthetics and form. The same spirit – or *Zeitgeist* – in which the house was built also guided the hand that conceived and planted the garden.

French "parterres" come to mind here, since they employ even more formal garden constructions to arrange both small townhouse

gardens or large-scale stately grounds, such as at the Château de Villandry.[16] And yet how different our relationship is with such (French) gardens compared to an English garden, where plants are afforded ample space to grow in character. Admittedly, a French-style parterre garden can be most appealing, going a long way toward satisfying the human desire for order. With regard to planting, however, such a "love" of order is somewhat oppressive, quite unlike an English garden where the human will to establish form yields to a more immediate relationship with the active nature of plantlife. Both garden designs evince entirely different attitudes toward nature. Yet if we are to arrive at a symbolic understanding of the trinity "house – garden – free nature," we must examine more closely what distinguishes gardens from houses and from vast, undomesticated nature, with its fields, forests, mountains, and lakes.

Houses are firm, permanent, enclosed structures, arising from human culture to meet human needs. If clothes are our second skin,

then houses are a strong and tough third skin protecting us against the elements and other dangers. They constitute an interior that provides security and peace, and seclusion from the outside world. Importantly, a roof closes off a house toward the sky and a cellar floor toward the earth. As noted, houses are entirely covered with skin.

Hence, houses often symbolize the human body. For example, the phrase "He or she is a bit weak in the upper storey" indicates that the brain is compared to the uppermost part of a house. Here, the distinction between an attic or garret and a cellar comes to mind: the former, (that is, the top of the house) is often dry; this is where the wind, often identified with the human intellect, wafts through the timberwork. It is also where we store matters of the mind, such as keepsakes, "souvenirs," old books, pictures, photographs, clothes, and other items that conjure up the past. By contrast, the cellar, or

belly of the house, is cool and slightly moist, well suited to storing foodstuffs and wine.

Perhaps your mind is now wandering through your own house, dear Reader, or through your parents' or grandparents' house, and you remember boxes containing items long forgotten or shelves full of apples, bottles covered in dust, and cleanly labeled bottling jars. While those forgotten items will now appear in your mind's eye, the contents of the bottles and the luscious fruit will probably whet your appetite.

Thus, a house can be likened to the human body in symbolic terms; it sometimes relates explicitly to the body but mostly with the structure of human consciousness, because it is always linked to the prevailing *Zeitgeist* and the technical and aesthetic knowledge and skills of its builders and occupants. Notably, a house is neither simply a natural hollow nor a pregnant woman's tummy, but a consciously constructed edifice. Even the smallest hut is built by hand and with "brains."

Thus, we refer to "thought constructs" or "mental structures," given our preference for organized and stable reflections and thought systems, or else these become visionary projects or sheer castles in the air. Outer and inner buildings are not subject to natural growth like trees but require deliberate construction. Considering one of his important dreams about houses, Carl Gustav Jung observed in his memoirs: "It was plain to me that the house represented a kind of image of the psyche – that is to say, of my then state of consciousness...."[17]

In our dreams, for example, houses are related to culture, the *Zeitgeist*, a particular *attitude* or *state of awareness*, in both a literal and figurative sense. In what follows I would like to illustrate this point.

If we dream about celebrating a feast in a magnificent Renaissance castle, the setting perhaps suggests that we yearn for a sensuous, ostentatious occasion conducted in the spirit of flourishing trade, considerable wealth, and thriving Renaissance liberal arts, outstanding painting and architecture. In any event, our dream transports us into the frame of mind of a Renaissance prince.

Or we retreat to a small "signalman's house," perhaps because we have grown tired of our expansive, turbulent household and instead long for restraint, simplicity, and silence. Should this small house assume the shape of a cell in our dreams or fantasies (or indeed in reality), and if it opens out onto a small, walled garden, a "hortus conclusus," we have in symbolic terms entered cloistral seclusion, a place devoted to the quest for knowledge and enlightenment. Our habitat is now restricted to the all important and most essential; this primordial space consists of a just about adequately sized interior, a small house large enough to pursue the inner quest, and an outer space, a garden, to explore and recognize the "Other" lying outside our personality. Our search for self-knowledge, knowledge of the world, or experience of God should not be directed merely inward but needs to turn toward the Other, the "Thou" and that which lies outside of us.

While these two spaces in the second image represent two opposite movements of body and soul, they form an essential part of the complete human being: one curls up and retreats inward, and the other opens up and outward, stretching its arms, hands, and face toward the sky and light. The flowers and plants growing in the small garden also open and reach upward toward the light, whereas the house repeats the enveloping, inward-turning movement. Both are like a person opening and closing their eyes, with an outward and then an inward gaze.

Thus, one of the essential differences between a prison cell and a Carthusian monk's cell is the small garden attached to the latter. Depriving an individual of a view of the sky and nature is probably one of the worst forms of punishment. (I seriously doubt whether such punishment can be helpful, for nothing is more likely to heal the human mind and soul, and rebalance them more effectively, than green, blooming nature and a vast open sky.)

Let us return to the juxtaposition of house and nature and the garden in-between. The counterpart of a house is the unbounded exterior, unrestrictedly open toward heaven and earth – the natural world, consisting of fields, forests, lakes, rivers, and so forth. None of these elements is man-made. Nature is not static or fixed like a house, but subject to constant flux and movement. It lives according to its own laws and forever eludes human domination. Nature originates in a creative power whose wisdom, beauty, splendor, and horror infinitely exceed human knowledge and skills. Even though the sciences continue to explore nature, and have significantly expanded our knowledge and awareness, it remains the great unknown. Both in symbolic and human terms, nature as the great unconscious is thus still the counterpart of the house as a creation of human consciousness.

Between these poles – that is, the vastness of unconscious nature and the house as part of human culture – lies the garden, that very particular *interstice*: it is not only a part of culture and nature, and it is not exclusively edifice or wilderness, but the *space in-between*, connecting these elements. Gardens also connect heaven and earth or

the upperworld and underworld for, as noted, their vertical dimension is neither closed nor bounded. By extension, they also connect the immutable and mutable, the fixed and mobile, such as a stony stairs and walls and sprawling, active growth. Gardens are the vessel in which the most diverse and contrasting elements converge and are conjoined.

Gardens stage a continuous back and forth between the devising, building, ordering, fantasizing, loving, or hating individual and nature, which responds to the range of human activity in its distinct manner, subject to its own rules and antics. The more affectionately we feel our way into nature's unknown essence, the more harmonious our garden becomes. Its totality is a microcosm and thus affords the individual an opportunity to take part in the greatness of creation on a small human scale.

This aspect of the garden leads me to the biblical account of the divine creation, and thus to another trinity than "cultural being – garden – nature," namely "God – man – garden." What becomes immediately apparent is that God has taken the place of Nature. The association of divine wisdom and nature's tremendous creative power is close to my heart, for how else could gardens be so dear to me?

In the story of creation, we read in Genesis, Chapter Two: "These *are* the generations of the heavens and of the earth when they were created, in the day that the Lord God made the earth and the heavens. / And every plant of the field before it was in the earth, and every herb of the field before it grew: for the Lord God had not caused it to rain upon the earth, and *there was* not a man to till the ground. / But there went up a mist from the earth, and watered the whole face of the ground. / And the Lord God formed man *of* the dust of the ground, and breathed into his nostrils the breath of life; and man became a living soul. / And the Lord God planted a garden eastward in Eden; and there he put the man whom he had formed."[18] The Bible then mentions four streams originating in Eden. That is, there is ample water and abundant fertility. Hence, most gardens modeled upon the Garden of Eden either contain a well or watering place that branches into four streams.

A few lines later we learn more about God's plan, and this strikes me as very important: "And the Lord God took the man, and put him into the garden of Eden to dress it and to keep it." Thus, God created a body out of the earth, an inner realm, into which he then breathed the breath of life, filling it with soul (as the Bible phrases it, a living soul). Subsequently, God created an external realm, the garden, in which plants and animals and human life could develop, and which human beings were allowed to, or even had to, protect and cultivate.

Space was created twice: once, as I see it, to provide the human soul with a place of residence; and a second time to afford the human soul the opportunity to enter into a relationship with the "other," or external nature, in order to develop and cultivate the garden and itself. Thus, the garden was of Eros, related both to the inner and outer world.

We can also reimagine the primordial situation of the story of creation thus: the soul moves back and forth between planet Earth or rather between the enclosed small earthen house and the open garden, half inside and outside at the same time, interweaving an inward gaze and one directed toward the world outside. Such an arrangement of the animated interior and exterior spaces once more recalls the cloistral cell and its small garden. Here, God's creative power, which animated the world from its primordial beginning, is sought and reexperienced once again, in both the interior and exterior, in the inner and outer worlds.

It seems to me that this quest for lines of communication leading back to the divine origin represents a path in both our soul and the world that Jungian depth psychology refers to as the process of individuation. I conceive individuation thus: to become that individual whom we were supposed to become – in relation to both the world within us and the world around us. What such a concise statement involves is in fact an interminably difficult and long developmental process. The process of becoming, of changing and assuming shape, involves perpetual movement back and forth between the inner world, or our individual dispositions, so to speak, and the outer world, our surroundings, the strange, the completely Other, which we ultimately call God.

The longer we pursue this process, the more we recognize that the outer and inner are not really dissociated. It only seems thus to us until we learn to gaze simultaneously inward with one eye and outward with the other. What emerges is that peculiar gaze that I thought to have observed on the faces of the visitors strolling around the Alcazar gardens in Seville (see Chapter 1). Thus, gardens are also the way of inner and outer work, of change and knowledge.[19]

But let us leave these deliberations aside for a moment and return to the "small soul garden" that God gifted us with, as I observed in commenting on the passage from Genesis above. No matter how small it is, every plot of earth that we are allowed to "dress and keep" constitutes a gift, for it links us to the completely Other that is not part of our ego consciousness.

I once lived in a historic district for a couple of years, high above the town with a view of old roof tiles, a church spire, and cobblestones. How much those four flower cases in which I grew flowers and herbs meant to me at the time! Each plant allowed me to share in the secret of growth and withering, and the beauty, joy, and sensuousness of nature. What was, and remains, true for me probably also holds true for you. Each plant teaches us patience and observation, astonishment and respect, joy and sometimes grief; and when it stands in our flowerpot or garden it demands our love, understanding, and care. It can bestow upon us confidence in the power of nature, and thus in life. May I encourage you to take a moment to feel your way toward your relationship with plants. Do you also experience this give-and-take between your plants and yourself? Do you sense just how much vitality emanates from these plants and flowers?

I would like to report a small, unforgettable incident from my days as a practising child therapist. I returned to my little practice after the summer holidays, accompanied by a small, timid boy whose soul was badly damaged. Upon entering the room, we discovered something special. Some sand had evidently clogged the drain of the old stone sink and a sunflower seed had somehow nestled there. Over the summer holidays, a small somewhat pale sunflower had grown from the seed, and its modest bloom now reached up toward the light. My little patient and I were very moved by the small flower's force, which had helped it grow "out of the gutter," as it were. He called it his "power flower."

I wish to add some further reflections on the great gardens. In most regions of the West, we are used to gardens that surround houses, which thus stand inside gardens. In southern and Arab countries, however, gardens often lie concealed behind towering walls or are situated within a house. Houses thus surround gardens, thereby concealing them from view. In Central Europe, we mostly afford passers-by a view of our garden. Strolling through a village is often a wonderful experience, delighting our eyes, nose, and heart. In the South, and even more so in Arab countries, we often find ourselves walking between walls and are left to fantasize about the concealed beauty lying behind them; on rare occasions, we might catch a glimpse of a splendid interior through a gate that happens to be open, or a bush or tree hanging over a wall kindles our imagination.

I wonder whether these different arrangements have anything to do with how northern and southern peoples open, disclose, or close their soul. The contrary seems to be the case at first sight. We would probably assume that people in northern countries tend to be more withdrawn while their southern counterparts are more open and spontaneous, "wearing their heart on the sleeve" so to speak. Yet if we consider that until a few centuries ago most houses and gardens were planned and built by men, we will probably only come nearer to an answer if we search for the "small garden" in the male psyche in order then to decide whether northern and southern males handle the matter differently.

I have often heard men refer to their beloved, or her most intimate femininity, as a "small garden." Presumably they mean that their beloved

is or has "a garden" in which they can take their walks and "engage in courtly love." But matters could also be different in that the erotic relationship with their beloved allows them to keep and cultivate their own "nature's little garden," that is, their urges, emotions, and feelings. At least I hope that men first attend to "their own garden"; for if they considered their beloved as a garden which they can treat and shape at whim, I would be inclined to express reservations about such a "garden culture."

But if one considers how much love and devotion many men put into planting, protecting, and keeping their outer garden, then one may hope that they will apply themselves similarly to cultivating their inner garden. And if we think about those innumerable enchanting and splendid gardens planted all over the world by men, we recognize these as marvelous gifts for all humanity, most probably arising from a rich and cultivated emotional world. How these feelings are subsequently expressed toward others, whether grandiloquently in ostentatious castle gardens or amiably in simple municipal gardens or subtly in delightful courtyard gardens, depends entirely on individual circumstances as well as circumstances of climate or the prevailing *Zeitgeist*, which also govern emotional worlds and thus the inner and outer garden. The fact that hardly any two gardens are alike suggests how individual inner or outer gardens are. Likewise, no two soul gardens are identical.

The relation between gardens and the world of feelings returns me to the meaning I attribute to the endopsychic landscape of house, garden, and vast nature. As mentioned at the beginning of this chapter, a house represents an individual's conscious personality. By contrast, I consider free, unspoiled nature and the surroundings beyond the garden to be the foreign, the Other, our unconscious nature. The garden would hence be the interstice occupying the area between human consciousness and our unconscious nature. It would be the place of encounter, exchange, and connection between both spheres, where unconscious nature can be rendered conscious, transformed, and thus cultivated.

Gardens are also the space in which therapeutic or personality enhancing, psychological work occurs, and in which a constructive dialogue between consciousness and the unconscious (such as the content of dreams) is aspired to. Generally speaking, it is also a sphere of play and creativity, for it is precisely in play that conscious and unconscious elements blend best, and where the creative individual allows ideas and inspirations to flow from the sphere of the unconscious into the "garden" where our consciousness assimilates and shapes these into something new.

In what follows, I would like to describe this process of change and refinement in the mixing vessel of the soul garden in closer detail. Our unconscious sides requiring change and cultivation reside in urges, emotions, feelings, thoughts, and their related inner images. Our soul garden consists of countless small and large inner images, which – shaped out of sense perceptions and thoughts – act as the carriers of emotions and feelings or, put differently, are interwoven with feelings. As far as we know, such energetically charged images already exist in some primordial form in children from the outset, or they form very early on. They develop and change as we grow older, always in terms of an interrelation between the inner and outer worlds. Images and feelings come and go, and flourish and wither like flowers. Some are looked after, refined, and cultivated to the point of significant sources of spiritual power and conscious knowledge.

Others, however, are neglected, left to grow wild, and relapse into the unconscious.

During the course of life, such images change and develop; in the most favorable case, emotions are "domesticated," and feelings refined and differentiated. Spiritual wealth emerges that can nurture and carry us through life. Not only are we thus animated, but so are our fellows, for example through creative work, as the visible and audible expression of spiritual wealth. In such instances, the biblical image – of the soul garden as the fount of life branching out in all directions – comes true.

In negative cases, the inner images disappear, the emotional world atrophies or petrifies, and the soul garden runs dry and becomes a spiritual desert. Moreover, a soul garden might close up and become surrounded by such high and thick walls that others can only intimate the feelings locked up behind them, catching only occasional whiffs of fragrance. How many, enticed by such fragrance, have bashed their heads against stone walls! And when they have finally dug a small hole through the wall, they catch sight of a solitary prickly shrub of fear and resistance, from which perhaps one forlorn rose is desperately emitting its fragrance into the sky and over the wall ...

Normally, however, a person's anima consists of many emotional, spiritual images that form, as it were, the intangible yet perceptible soul garden, the energy field or fluid surrounding the body house. Like the flowers and trees surrounding our houses and giving others a first impression of who we are, the expression of feelings and our emotionality form the space connecting others and our own existence.

The fluid emanating from one person's spiritual world or their soul garden's fragrance and sound, to phrase it in the imagery of the garden, attracts, repels, enchants, obfuscates, or appeals to us so much that we wish to discover that garden. We are often curious or desirous enough, but discovering a foreign soul garden is an adventure that can also evoke great fear. For this is where many unknown plants grow. Most of this growth is strange and uncanny, and it requires courage to advance further.

But the owners of gardens are also afraid, fearing for their plants; they hence plant thorny hedges or attempt to confuse the intruder with sweetly fragrant blossoms and poisonous seeds. That is, they adopt either a deterrent bristly and aggressive stance or attempt to confuse the intruder with sweet ado and fuss or ensnaring talk. Opening our soul garden to someone else, on the other hand, bears witness to inner certainty and trust – or else to great naivety. Gardens and psychic states offer themselves to endless comparison, and we all are able to devise our own games in this respect.

We have meanwhile arrived at the interrelation between two soul gardens (see Chapter 6). We all constitute the strange unknown for others; the "You" becomes the wilderness, so to speak. Others represent the essentially foreign, and we all protect our souls. Soul gardens can draw nearer to each other only very slowly and cautiously until they are close enough to connect.

A few examples will serve to illustrate this point. For instance, the symbolism "familiar house – unfamiliar wilderness and a garden in-between" translates into "familiar, conscious personality – the world of the unconscious and the soul garden in-between." What occurs in this space in-between? Let us assume that undefinable, bleak fears emerge from our unconscious. These are like ugly, poisonous plants that crawl toward and over our garden fence from the wilderness. We would like to rid ourselves of these fears, but they cling to us like burs and resist detachment.

We cannot simply douse these poisonous fears with herbicide like undesirable weeds in the outer garden. We probably first attempt to deny these fears and banish them from view. We look across at our neighbor's garden only to avoid apprehending our own fearsome plants. We do this and that to dispose of them, but to no avail. Ultimately, we accept them; that is, we bring them closer to ourselves to have a better view. For there is little use in poisoning our fears and throwing them on the dung heap. They survive even the worst weeds.

But if we inquire into what we really fear, and what stuff our fears are made of, just as we would more closely examine an unknown, initially fear-evoking plant, these gradually assume a recognizable form and can be deciphered and processed. Closer observation means to overtly address an issue or object, without prejudice, so that it may speak to us and reveal its nature. Such engagement entails a back and forth between the ego and the other, the known and the unknown. This process of change occurs in the vessel of the soul garden. We become familiar with the undesired plant or the terrible fears, and these lose their power over us and can perhaps even assume permanent residence in our garden – in which we can observe them.

My second example is somewhat more cheerful for it concerns a small love story. It is about two soul gardens, two personalities, with a certain self-awareness, and two worlds of the unconscious.

Let us imagine a young man called Retterich (in German, the name derives from "radish" not from "retten" – to save or rescue). While he has a rough-and-ready notion of himself, he, too, has a spiritual world. Those around him, in particular females, continue to confound him. Yet he senses a strong desire for the opposite sex, which has remained unexplored so far. Retterich is adventurous. One day, on one of his peregrinations, a scent suggesting a thousand roses suddenly approaches him; or perhaps it was an old perfume known as "N'aimez que moi" or possibly some other bearing an auspicious name; no matter, because Retterich cannot help following the fragrance.

It lures him into a small garden. He peeps over the fence curiously and discovers one of the most beautiful flower gardens imaginable. Flowers are abloom and seem even more beautiful – or at least as beautiful – as those in the magnificent still-lives of the Dutch masters. Or as those scattered lightly and seductively on the spring meadow and Flora's dress in Botticelli's painting *Primavera* (c. 1482), where the nymph Chloris even breathes a rose, which can be seen growing from her mouth.[20]

Retterich is so completely enchanted by such abundant sense-delighting femininity that he at first fails to notice a small house and a real-life young woman standing in the garden. Is this Rosa? Or is she called Margerita? Veronica, Viola, or perhaps Begonia? Or is this possibly love-in-a-mist or busy lizzie? It is amazing just how many female names are related to flowers. Well, as a matter of fact, it is not, but

quite simply natural. Women and flowers belong together. I recently came across an instructive dream in this respect:

> *A woman dreamt she was in an old, rustic building in the South. All of a sudden, two figures came towards her across the farmyard: a plain, small countrywoman and her husband. The woman stepped up to the dreamer and with a nice gesture offered her a small glass vase containing a small branch of Gypsophila. On presenting the vase, the woman said: "Dal mio stemma" – from my stock, from my root. The dreamer was delighted and asked why she was being given the present. The man replied: "Perche le donne sono come le rose" – because women are like roses; and as he uttered these words, the dreamer saw that he delicately clasped a small, red rose in his hands.*

*

Thus, let us call the young woman in the magic garden Rosa. She obviously invites Retterich to enter the garden, not immediately

but following some initial pleasantries which serve to break the ice. She shows him all her flowers, the roses, carnations, violets, zinnias, tagetes, and sunflowers; the gypsophila, tickseed, cosmos, salvias, and all the star gladiolus bearing the scent of cinnamon and other spices. Retterich is mesmerized; all these flowers, colors, forms, and scents are so foreign to him, just as foreign as the playful and self-enamored young woman. And yet somewhere a chord strikes within him: does he not know all this, too? Did his soul garden contain niches with flowers and summer birds?

Nothing would please him more than to live with the flower girl forever. Rosa, too, is curious. She would like to become acquainted with Retterich's garden, and hopes to discover flowers and bushes she has never seen before. She sets off in buoyant and hopeful spirits, while he accompanies her somewhat hesitantly for he senses that his garden will perhaps not quite satisfy her expectations. And thus it is. Where are the delicate, pastel-color, bright flowers? What about the butterflies? And what about the alluring fragrances?

Retterich's garden is a kitchen garden, replete with carrots, cucumbers, radishes, beans (which have served flirting very well ever since Wilhelm Busch, but which also grow tall and have ambition) as well as potatoes, cauliflowers, and other life-sustaining vegetables. In one corner a juicy clover grows for the rabbit, but what beauty does clover have to offer?[21]

The otherness of Retterich's garden fascinates Rosa at first. Even though its many male vegetables attract her, she becomes more and more disappointed and vexed. "Male soul gardens are merely rational, boring, and determined by need," she grumbles. If she were called Viola, she might consider the carrots and cauliflowers beautiful and tie them into her bouquet, as many florists do nowadays. But not Rosa. She bristles and thinks: "This Retterich. I will show him how a woman plants a proper garden. This will make a proper man of him."

Indeed, fate then runs its course. Rosa feverishly sets to work in Retterich's garden, planting flowers and blooming bushes, sowing, trimming, watering it – unaware that soon only she is keeping it while Retterich slowly withdraws. He feels overtaken by events and alien.

His garden, now no longer really his own, no longer interests him, and he soon turns to planting his cucumbers in the asbestos flowerpots in the open-plan office at work. He had been so enchanted by *Rosa's* garden after all. What has happened to it since? It has withered, grown desolate and boring, because Rosa has applied all her energy to his garden – or rather turned the space within *his* fence into *her* garden.

Turnips and carrots, roses and lilies, now grow topsy-turvy: two formerly different, yet very appealing soul gardens have become a spiritual desert and an alienated soul garden. Neither Rosa nor Retterich has any inclination to visit the other's garden. They look across garden fences into other gardens, choose rose fragrances from the gardening catalog, and purchase their vegetables at the supermarket. Sometimes Rosa wistfully recalls Retterich's beans and radishes that had tasted so much better after all. And Retterich longs for Rosa's "unuseful" bouquets, which served no other purpose than to please.

The story could have taken a different course: Rosa and Retterich both could have remembered what had once been theirs and what it was about the other's garden that had fascinated them or nurtured them for a good long while. Each would have then returned to their soul garden and deliberated: he to ponder whether he wished to live without the playful, seductive, erotic feelings that her flowers expressed; and she to consider whether she could survive without his life-sustaining, wholesome vegetables, that is, their down-to-earth, matter-of-fact energy.

Yet as the story in fact played out, it was no longer a fairy tale but an account of an everyday relationship. Neither has entered the other's garden with adequate caution and due love. Neither has realized that the garden is merely a world in-between both. The other, however, is a stranger whose psychological structure they must empathize with slowly and arduously.

Nature cunningly engineers initial, mutual attraction by surrounding our beloved with exactly the kind of soul garden we desire for ourselves. Our fantasy subsequently attributes miracles – and flowers

– to our beloved, and vice versa, and we perceive them as ourselves. Psychology calls this process "projection." Nature's ruse strikes me as both useful or even necessary to throw two people together in the first place. Failing the playfulness of projection, human beings might perhaps be too alien or too afraid of each other. Thus nature, that cunning witch, paints bright spiritual ideals around strangers that are so enchanting that we fall madly in love on the spot.

Later, a lot of hard work is involved in distinguishing the ideal and the other's real garden. It is equally hard work to shape our ideal garden within the confines of our garden such that we do not need to keep attempting to find it in yet another person. Rosa will have to learn to plant vegetables beside dancing, fragrant flowers to avoid suffering spiritual death. For his part, Retterich must plant flowers to be able to express his feelings with his own bouquets, so that he need not trouble Rosa whenever he wishes to gift someone with a bunch of flowers.

Both can now attend to their own, more complete garden. Will this not become horribly boring? Do Rosa and Retterich still need each other? I believe they do. For now they can plant a third garden, a common one that only they share, a lovers' garden in which she dances for him and he cooks for her – or vice versa.

Chapter Four

A Garden Stroll from Morning to Evening: Roses and Carnations, Flowers and Clouds

In my youth, I used to spend the summer holidays with my brothers, sisters, and cousins in our grandparents' paradisal garden out in the country – a labor-intensive paradise, however, that also spelled much work for us children. Grandfather would read the newspaper at breakfast until small chickadees would disturb him. They knew that he always had pine nuts in his pockets, and relished playing their game with him until they had eaten the very last nut out of his hand. He then rose and said to me: "C'mon, let's go into the garden!" I knew exactly where he wanted to take me – over to the garden house in which many small carnation flowers bloomed and gave off a beguiling fragrance from afar. And thus as a little girl I would walk around the garden with my grandfather, learning so much about flowers, herbs, and trees. His favorite tree was a beautiful gnarled quince tree, whose significance occurred to me only much later when it reappeared in a dream.

In this dream I stood in my grandparents' garden again. The house was being pulled down, but the garden remained untouched. My task was to conserve my grandfather's quince tree and the sick children's drawings that he had begun collecting during his time as a pediatrician at the children's hospital.

*

This dream came to me a good thirty-five years after those morning walks with my grandfather. It was a highly significant dream, which we will encounter again in Chapter 8. What matters for the moment is how early in life meaningful experiences take hold, only to recur later in our dreams in adult life, pointing us in directions evidently chalked out much earlier. The pattern in our life's carpet is established very early on, except that we are often blind to it for a long time.

As mentioned, my grandfather was a medical doctor. He loved nature on account of its beauty and healing power. His relationship with nature was profoundly religious; for him, God was above all manifest in nature, which I understood only when I was no longer a little girl and he was very old. Those walks with my grandfather, however, shaped my relationship with nature decisively from early childhood as well as my interest in the relations among the plant and animal worlds and the human body, soul, and mind.

I attach great significance to children spending time in a garden with their parents or grandparents, jointly observing nature and engaged in learning and working. It is not enough for a child's biological mother or attachment figure to be "good and well meaning." Developing trust in the world requires a good relationship with the earth on which a child stands, as much as with its closer and wider surroundings. Thus, "it takes a whole village to raise a child," as a meaningful American proverb phrases it. Being familiar with the people, animals, trees, and plants in its surroundings contributes decisively to a child's orientation, security, and rootedness in the world – and indeed in life – and so does its knowledge of the course of the sun, moon, and stars.

In what follows, I wish to consider Maria, an eight-year-old girl whose therapeutic process I discussed in my account of the sandplay method, to illustrate how important the transition from a biological mother to great Mother Nature is.[22] Over the course of therapy, Maria developed a very strong bond with me, and I became a kind of second mother to her. These strong feelings for me slowly faded toward the end of therapy, as Maria instinctively headed out into the garden, that is, nature, in our last few sessions. Her adventurousness afforded us the opportunity to jointly observe, and hence establish a relationship with, the plants, birds, butterflies and the many other small creatures biding their time in the garden. Thus, her trust in me gradually shifted onto nature, the "great mother." This enlarged the scope of our joint undertaking, and Maria now stepped out confidently into the larger vessel of the human relationship with nature. Where would this transition have occurred any better than in the sheltering space of the garden?

Hence, it is wonderful when parents take the time to acquaint their children with nature, not only through showing them its beauty and force but also through *not* absolving them from the boring and arduous work involved. Young people thus learn that keeping a garden, tilling its soil, and weeding and watering plants require time and patience but ultimately bear fruit. Whoever has learned to appreciate and comprehend nature, that is, to cultivate a garden with love, will never assume that life is a paradisal garden in which flowers engulf us with fragrance and fruit always falls off trees straight into our mouths. How troublesome and difficult it is for adults to learn to come down to earth (literally!) from their delusions of grandeur and realize that a fruitful relationship with reality involves so much time, effort, and down-to-earth work!

This reminds me of the down-to-earth, primordial tortoise, one of the most significant symbolic animals. The tortoise advances slowly yet purposefully and instinctually. Its symbolic range is great; it occurs as the creator or bearer of the world in various mythologies, and thus has considerable archetypal meaning.[23] In my experience, its appearance in an individual's dreams of fantasies mostly suggests that a down-to-earth, stable process is underway in relation to the real world, allowing that person to progress slowly and modestly, yet unswervingly and imperturbably toward an objective, such as a new development.[24] Such step-by-step advancement – which the Italians refer to as "chi va piano, va sano" (who moves slowly, moves sanely) – overwhelms neither the tortoise nor the human being. Great tasks can be undertaken and accomplished thus, such as tending, and working hard for, a garden.

Let us also advance, in our case toward the destination of those walks in my grandparents' garden: the full bed of carnations. Since my nose and eyes were even closer to the fragrance and blaze of colors, I was allowed to choose a particularly beautiful flower, which my grandfather would then put in his buttonhole. It was actually a small erotic game, giving expression to the affection between the old man and the little girl. For me, as observed above, this small flower, and its symbolic meaning, prefigured a crucial development later in my life; for my grandfather, it was probably a small, fragrant "flower of emotion."

Various paintings of the old masters aptly illustrate the symbolism of the carnation. Jan van Eyck's "Portrait of a Man with Carnation," for instance, depicts a quite unappealing and rather coarse fellow holding a delicate, tiny bunch of carnations which affords him a touching sense of charm.[25]

Hans Holbein the Younger's "Portrait of the Merchant Georg Gisze" shows the merchant sitting at a table upon which stands a crystal vase containing a bunch of carnations, rosemary, hysop, and a plain yellow flower, among various other objects. The plants indicate, symbolically, the depicted person's attributes and virtues: love, loyalty, purity, and modesty. In particular the carnations, as a symbolic allusion to love and loyalty, suggest that the portrait was commissioned on the occasion of Gisze's engagement to Christine Krüger.[26] Considered thus, the painting portrays an engagement, and the carnations convey the future bride's feelings for her fiancé. The blooming flowers were ambassadors of the soul in

Holbein's day, just as they serve us nowadays to express our feelings for others through the most amazingly varied flower arrangements.

One of the Grimms' fairy tales bears the title "The Carnation." In this tale, a young man discovers, or rather conquers, his beloved in the magical world – that is, in the world of the imagination, where all is possible. At a certain point in the tale, he would like to lead her home into the real world of his father's castle. He asks her to accompany him, but she refuses. He implores her, but she still refuses. Without further ado, the young man turns his beloved into a carnation, puts the flower in his buttonhole, and sets off. Upon returning home, he gives the company at table an account of his experiences in the other, magical world; he also mentions that he has found his true love. They laugh and disbelieve him. He pulls the carnation out of his pocket and places it on the table – and behold, the flower turns back into a beautiful young woman.[27]

Flowers are closely associated with expressions of love and feelings, as we all know, and carnations in particular used to be popular ambassadors of love. Carnations are much less popular nowadays because breeding has overemphasized thick and pompous stems. By contrast, those small, splendidly fragrant specimens in my grandfather's garden, which flowered in all colors, were something else!

This brief account of the carnation holds the promise of a beautiful and happy summer's day. Its fragrance, moreover, enveloped my grandfather's rather dry scientific deskwork. At present I recall those days, thinking: "Oh yes, some wear carnations in their buttonhole, and others have a cup of coffee on their desks." Thus, we all build our own little bridges of pleasure to our toilsome chores.

The story of the carnation touches upon morning, the time of new beginning and hope. In terms of seasonal change, it would belong to spring. In Greek mythology, three aspects of the great goddess embodied the cycle of the year. Selene, the virginal goddess, represented *spring*, which was also likened to the waxing moon,[28] and is customarily associated with the color white. To my mind a blooming cherry tree best captures its essence, or bright, delicate, aqueous spring flowers, or even hopeful, light-green lime tree and birch leaves. With regard to human life, spring is the time of youth, that phase of life in which the first, yet still delicate, albeit hopeful patterns emerge in the carpet of life.

Noon, *summer*, the full moon, and the sexually fully mature female mark the time of Aphrodite or Venus. Fiery, passionate red roses fully abloom, and colorful, fragrant, erotic summer flowers and fruits are all part of her.

In her marvelous *Pagan Meditations: The Worlds of Aphrodite, Artemis, and Hestis*, Ginette Paris observes: "That Aphrodite, the Goddess of sexual love and beauty, is also the Goddess of flowers appears to me to be the kind of evidence one receives when mythical thought penetrates the mind: Are not flowers the most beautiful sexual organs of the universe? Many are the images and expressions which associate

the feminine sex with flowers and, above all, with the pink rose, rich in color and perfume, with outspread petals resembling the tenderness of flesh. To complete its participation in the myth of Aphrodite, the rose comes with painful thorns, which emphasize the risk of picking it, the suffering that comes with all sexual passions."[29]

In the next passage, she speaks from the bottom of my heart: "To be preoccupied with flowers or to create a pleasant garden, as to make love or to 'dress up' – these are all ways of honoring Aphrodite. Gardens express the sensuality of a culture, a type of sensuality that, for those whose educational background or age has caused them to ignore sexual vitality, offers the advantage of being without anxiety."[30]

As an enclosed, sheltered space, the garden affords us the opportunity to indulge in sensuality unencumbered by fear. Plants, too, are

essentially peaceful and yet they can be highly sensuous at the same time. Flowers and fruits are thus very well suited to experiencing sensuality unencumbered by fear. But not exclusively – or does their attraction not conceal a great deal more? Since they contribute so much to enjoying a garden, I devote the next chapter to the qualities of sensuousness, beauty and joy, and those aphrodisiacal forces abiding in them.

Beforehand, however, I would like to turn to another memory, one which bears evening, departure from life, and muted grieving within itself. A waxing moon and a dark empty moon, the color black, autumn and winter, deeply radiant autumn flowers, and the melancholy of lapsing, moldy autumn forests: these all befit Hecate, an old woman, the goddess of the wilderness, and an enlightened witch.[31]

Hecate evokes memories of my "grandmother's roses": a few years after picking carnations for my grandfather on our morning walks in the garden, I would accompany my grandmother to her roses in the evening. Unlike my grandfather, who sported a trademark debonair Maurice Chevalier-like straw hat, my grandmother would don a straw hat with its brim curved gently downward. She took a large basket and a pair of pruning shears and walked across to the long rose hedge. She would snip off the withered petals, carefully and patiently, and throw them into the basket. Whilst she did this, there was a lot of time to talk, but also much time and peace to *be* with her. I realized that such silent togetherness or quiet working side by side is conducive to a deep sense of affinity and attachment. I am often reminded of the feeling of deep, inner affinity that arises from silent togetherness when I accompany patients on their spiritual path.

I learned such tranquility from spending evenings at my grandmother's rose hedge or doing other chores around the house and garden with her. I also learned that the withered and sick need to be removed with great care so that plants can apply all their energy to growing new flowers. While much that we experience in a garden, such as different atmospheres, events, and chores, can be transferred onto the life of the human soul, it is very important to let go of and prune away entrenched forms of behavior, or those past due, so as to make way for fresh spiritual impulses. We must hence sometimes apply our soul garden shears somewhat forcefully to cut away long bygone and now unnecessary feelings of inferiority and complexes of abandonment to release energy for new tasks!

The old woman's wisdom inhered in what she had learned and experienced over many years: that where the single rose withers, decays, and becomes compost and earth, the plant buds and flowers anew. An incident from my own practice affirms how important it is to comprehend this process. One day one of my female patients, who again and again fixed upon an instance of culpable behavior in her life and hence repeatedly fell into the same, desperate depression, had the following dream:

She was walking along a path. A thin forest lay head of her in the sunlight. Behind and beside her the possibility of falling into a gloomy gorge. A voice spoke to her: "You must now go forward." From this day, she realized that her guilt was part of her life, but that she now had to look ahead so as not to continue hindering her further development.

*

I cannot leave unmentioned one important branch of the rose story: my grandmother would often not only cut off withered flowers but also give us girls particularly beautiful specimens of fully blossomed fragrant roses whose petals we placed in a small bowl of water in a sunny spot for a few days – the velvety, crimson ones were of course particularly treasured on account of their intoxicating fragrance. And thus our first perfume came to life, our own rose water.

Such childish-female behavior might amuse you, and yet behind it stood my growing awareness of Aphrodite, as much as did the ancient and state-of-the-art knowledge that both sweet fragrances and curative or poisonous essences can be extracted from blossoms and herbs. Often it is only a matter of quantity that makes an herbal medicine poisonous.

With regard to the association between garden and soul, it is noteworthy that many petal and herbal essences are applied not only to remedy physical ailments but also to positively affect the soul, for instance to act upon the soul and mind through the body as liquids or ointments. Valerian, melissa, or lavender, for instance, are used to soothe the body and psyche in the form of tea or drops; and there are innumerable plants to which a love-enhancing effect is attributed. Remedies and eroticism are inseparable, and fertility-enhancing substances blend with aphrodisiacs. Allegedly "benign" and common parsley is one such plant, as we will see, as well as artichoke, ginseng, lovage, and the very popular asparagus, among others.[32]

Nor should we forget intoxicating and poisonous plants, also known as the plants of the gods on account of their magic and mind-altering potency, for better or worse. These plants' prodigious, yet sometimes uncanny and destructive forces have always been considered sacred or demonic rather than commonplace and ordinary. Earlier, perhaps more responsibly-minded cultures than our present one treated these plants with great respect. They came down from the gods after all! Much more could be said here, but I will leave my readers to explore the herb and witch's garden.

Significantly, we are organic creatures, bearing an herbal and vegetable life within us, and thus capable of establishing a relationship with the forces active in flowers and herbs. Albertus Magnus already asserted in the thirteenth century during the reign of Frederick II that plants have souls, not a human but a plant soul. Magnus, a theologian, naturalist, Dominican friar, and bishop of Regensburg, revered Aristotle, who had already believed that plants have souls. Magnus's "De Vegetabilibus et Plantis," a great botanical treatise, comprises much philosophical deliberation on the plant world and a taxonomy of approximately 390 plant species, from trees to bushes, shrubs, and from herbs to fungi and mushrooms.

I wish to highlight one of Magnus's particularly interesting and original thoughts: his study of plants led him to believe that a plant resembled a human being stood upside down, since its root (that is, mouth) lies buried in the dark soil, facing downward and passively assimilating nutriments from its moist environment. He argued further that the root of a plant is its heart, which produces movement and bestows warmth on the juice absorbed. The warmth of the sun, he claimed, boosts the low temperature of plants, thereby promoting growth and proliferation. Some plants were voracious, others abstemious, and others were prone to sweat and rot easily.[33]

The image of a plant as an inverted human being is highly unusual. Or is it perhaps rather the image of a human being as a plant standing upside down? No matter – Magnus's conception prompts further deliberation on the relationship between human beings and plants. In any event, it is crucial not to brush aside the appearance of flowers and plants in dreams and fairy tales. Instead, we should ask ourselves: "What exactly is this 'weed' trying to tell me?" Thus, it is hardly accidental that the Basil Girl sits among basil in the eponymous fairy tale. Nor is it insignificant that the Rapunzel plant in the original version of Grimm's "Rapunzel" is not harmless Rapunzel lettuce but parsley which, depending on the amount, can be either an aphrodisiac or an abortifacient.[34] In the Italian fairy tale "Petrosinella" ("Parsley Girl"), an older, more cheerful version of the Rapunzel motif, the young maiden learns a great deal from the witch in the tower. The witch was evidently an "herbal witch," that is, nothing other than a woman steeped in knowledge about the nature and effects of herbs.

The witch teaches Petrosinella that the spangles in the tower possess magic powers. Thus, Sergius Golowin's remark that these spangles are presumably datura, the fruit of the *Datura stramonium*, is quite feasible.[35] Its seeds have a strong hallucinatory effect, capable of altering one's view of reality. (Notably, the Datura stramonium is also one of the gods' plants!) Equipped with this knowledge, Petrosinella dupes the witch, who had sought to prevent the maiden from escaping from the tower with her beloved. Petronsinella threw one datura after the other in the witch's path, and the apples turned into a "terrifying Corsican bulldog," a "dreadful lion," and a "wolf" that ultimately devoured the witch from head to toe.[36]

The Italian version of the fairy tale is not only much more amusing and zestful than the Grimms' Rapunzel, but it also teaches us that something must be paid back in kind. The witch teaches Petrosinella witchcraft, that is, the proper and effective handling of herbal agents.

The story of the rose began with my grandmother and ends with the witch. Quite rightly, since grandmothers are often witchlike – longevity imparts much knowledge, including the dark and abysmal side of the world. Or we recall Hecate, the ancient goddess, whose knowledge about what occurs above and beneath the earth is comprehensive: there is something Hecatean about most "grandmothers," for behind today's modern, youthful grandmothers stands an imperious and awe-inspiring dark woman, who carries ties to the unknown night of death. The poem below – "In the Garden at Night" – takes up this dark and sombre atmosphere and marks the transition from evening to night in the garden. The time of gradually increasing darkness has its own particular magic. The white flowers continue to shine for a long time, the smells become intoxicating and almost tangible, the air envelops us like a mysterious veil, and other sounds reach our ears – another garden superimposes itself onto our familiar image:

In the Garden at Night

A black garden at night,
The gravel scrunches softly underfoot.
A few stars twinkle,
most of them silently,
two or three with all their might.
The lawn smells sweet,
And the lilac bushes pungent.
Later the roses afar,
While a hand strokes the box hedge
and touches the small bristly wall
and the yews,
soft and untrimmed this year.
The garden sleeps and yet dreams aloud.
Standing still, one hears the foliage of the wood whisper.
An owl cries, thrice:
"Good night, friend of the Goddess. Good night."
Time to retire inside.

Time to sleep and dream. Yet – let morning return soon! Night draws back its mysterious veil at daybreak, and we see the world again – almost with clear eyes. We can now turn once more to the carnations, roses, violets, sunflowers, poppies, and all those other flowers that embellish the world. Flowers mean life. Every single flower has a soul; and each species of flower has its own distinct soul. Flowers are much more than we might assume.

Closely examining a flower affords us a stunning view of its transparent, delicate, moist, and almost fluid petals. These strike us as virtually ethereal and elfish. Swaying in the wind between heaven and earth, moreover, they appear to be no more than a whisper, and yet they are firmly rooted in the soil. Flowers are symbols for the overcoming of death, which comes to seeds in the earth, and their resurrection in new form. They represent not only the overcoming of death in elapsing and reblooming nature but also their delicate,

ethereal blossoms are an ancient image for life after death in a new, spiritual form.

In *On Dreams and Death*, Marie-Louise von Franz observes: "The idea of flowers as *prima materia* is present in the religious conception of the world of the Persians as the primary material of the resurrection process. As we see in Persian landscape representations of the Beyond, every angel and every divine power possesses its own special flower. The god Vohuman has the white jasmine, Shativar the basil, the Daena – the divine anima of the male – has the rose of a hundred petals. One meditates on these flowers in order to constellate their 'energies,' with which the angel or the divine force itself then illuminates the inner field of vision. Thus the meditation on a flower, as Henri Corbin expresses it, makes possible an epiphany of otherwordly divine beings within the archetypal world."[37]

Besides, we know that the ancient Egyptian concept of resurrection was associated with the image of the plant world, and that flowers were one aspect of the resurrection of the body. In ancient Egypt, flowers were placed on the face, hands, and feet of the dead, and wheat grains or flower bulbs were tucked into their mummy bandages or placed in a receptacle beside the corpse and doused with water. When the grains or bulbs germinated, this was considered a sign of accomplished resurrection.[38]

Osiris's funerary bed provides an excellent summary of the symbolism of life, death, and resurrection on a small scale. We need to imagine a wooden box, approximately 200 cm in length, offering a side view of Osiris, the ancient Egyptian god. The box was filled with fine quartz sand from the bed of the River Nile. It appears that the box was sown with barley because when Osiris's bed (one among many found in ancient Egyptian tombs) was discovered in Tutankhamen's tomb, it contained withered barley shoots measuring about eight centimeters. Quite evidently, the barley had germinated thousands of years ago and grown. The growth of barley symbolizes one of the key themes in the cult of Osiris: new life after death.[39]

In ancient Egyptian thinking, Osiris was the source and bearer of life. At the same time, he was the ruler of the kingdom of the dead and the waters of the Nile, and thus ruler over all existence. In a hymn

that has survived on a papyrus scroll held at the Louvre in Paris, it says: "O Osiris, thou who leadest those of the Western Lands! Thou renewest thyself each day on the sky's rim, and growest old when the time cometh. The Nile riseth at thy behest, and thou feedest the people with that which flows from thy limbs, and makest all the fields wax when thou comest, when thou swellest and cometh to thy rest. Thy waters make the plants green."[40]

Osiris is the god of growth, and of life and death; he is the god of greening and decay, and governor of the world and existence. Thus, we return to autumn and winter in the garden. Autumn storms sweep the leaves from the trees; green turns into yellow-red-brown and finally disappears under a blanket of snow. The time of dormancy has arrived. Nature appears to have reached a standstill and death, but in actual fact this is not true. We fail to see, just as so much eludes us, since we are prone to short-term thinking. In the seed and grain, however, new life prepares its arrival during dormancy. Before long, the spring sunlight will awaken the "sacred green power," and the color green, the other bright colors, and the carnations and roses will all soon return to the garden.

Chapter Five

Beauty, Joy, and Sensuousness: Gifts from Gardens to Humanity

Almost every garden can be a magic garden or even a garden of love, tempting us to sensuousness, joy, eroticism, even sexuality. Yet to perceive the enchanting and magical nature of the garden, and to recognize therein the animated world in-between, calls for a particular point of view. We need what I would call a double eye, one eye that looks outward to the here and now, and another that simultaneously looks inward to the world of memories, stories, myths, fairy tales, and their multilayered spiritual backgrounds. These two eyes can interact, influence one another, and complement and alter a possibly one-sided view of matters.

Let us assume that a person's outer eye caught sight of a rose – not so much consciously, but a fleeting, ephemeral glimpse. Memories and images arise rapidly before the inner eye and cluster around the theme of the rose. Perhaps the images before the inner eye are shaped so as to cling painfully to the rose's thorns – and only the thorns. This one-sided perspective is subjectively tinted, evoking a thorny and hurtful notion; in objective terms, however, the outer eye has never beheld a rose closely enough to have gained adequate knowledge about it. He or she will entertain an entrenched, subjective opinion, perhaps even the fixed idea that roses are nothing but "thorny."

We are, of course, familiar with such one-sided, negative views from other areas of life, completely apart from roses: for example, for some people all women are "overmothering" while for others all men are "soulless"; equally, "black is beautiful," "white forever ugly," and all others "forever evil." But it could be that a fortunate moment occurs (perhaps prompted by someone else) in which the outer eye beholds the thorns more closely, and wanders along the thorny stem, perhaps discovering for the first time the bloom that is neither spiky nor pain-inducing, but soft, delicate, and wonderful. The outer eye now recognizes the rose in its entirety, consisting of both the spiky thorns and the delicate, fragrant flower. Recognizing both the positive *and* negative as well as external features often shifts inner perception in that a formerly one-sided view evolves into a more balanced, holistic one.

The opposite can also occur. Someone knows the name of a particular rose, and knows how to cut, fertilize, and tie it. His outer eye loves and appreciates roses. But that is as far as it goes. This, too, is a one-sided view, since he will have never discerned the rose goddess in the background, nor read the poetry, fairy tales, and stories entwining it. He will have never contemplated which roses mirror his partner's nature, for instance, and so will have never presented her with a bunch of those very roses. And yet she (the friend or the rose?) would be grateful. His inner eye is quite simply not yet conscious.

And yet one day, once again in a fortunate moment — such instances occur precisely when a person has become mature enough to recognize and embrace them — some minor circumstance opens up his inner eye, and all of a sudden, his world redoubles. The alert double eye enriches us!

In my experience, opening the inner eye not only enriches, but also invigorates and animates us. I have also observed that closely beholding external phenomena with the outer eye bears significantly on our inner perception, obviously in both negative and positive terms. It can cloud our soul or enlighten and bless it. Both as a psychotherapist and as an individual experiencing and observing the world, I endeavor to open up the inner eye of others towards the wealth of the soul, and to invite them to join my quest for positive, outer values capable of compensating and changing the widespread bleak and depressed inner view, that can also make us ill.

The garden is one such value, and within it "beauty," "sensuousness," and, of course, "pleasure," their divine companion. I also know that one great goddess informs these three "graces"; once we have experienced and discerned this goddess in the world outside, she becomes a most profound, life-enhancing value. She is the goddess of love and life, embodying the love of creation. Yet she has dangerous and destructive antagonist, namely evil inimical tendencies towards love and life, residing neither in plants nor animals, but within us. The more aware I become of destructive and life-inimical evil, the more I seek out the goddess of life, love, and joy.

In slowly approaching this goddess, I first wish to entice you to play, fantasize, and imagine! Please imagine a garden. Is not the sheer fact amazing that we can conjure up a garden before our mind's eye? Is it not astonishing that we are able to resurrect those gardens we once knew, and also erect new ones, entirely in our imagination?

How truly wonderful this imaginative force is! It enables us to sit at a typewriter with open eyes while our mind's eye conjures up the most magnificent gardens. We behold the flowers abloom in this garden with our inner eye, and can touch them, while imagining their fragrance is somewhat more difficult. We will not hear the plants, since this would require very alert ears, a sixth sense so to speak ... and yet our mind's eye hears the birdsong, the crickets chirping, the wind rustling in the tree-tops, the rain pattering on the stone slabs. We can also conjure up the taste of ripe blackberries or, heaven forbid, an unripe olive. It is all in the mind, a matter of the imagination!

Yet how much more intense is such sensory perception

when experienced for real in the garden, perhaps on a spring morning or a summer evening! How these sensual, erotic impressions surge towards us!

In spring, for instance, hundreds of small white blooms enshroud the black-thorn bush, and in their wake come innumerable, ever so delicate cherry blossoms, always five petals entwined around the golden or reddish filaments. Five – the number of Ishtar, the goddess of fer-tility, our Aphrodite-Venus, the goddess of love.[41] How could it be any different, for she is the great goddess of the garden besides Flora. The figure five recurs throughout the garden, such as the pentagrammic petals and leaves that echo the nature of the goddess at every turn. She, who was born from the sea, is also said to have stepped ashore in Kypros, or Cyprus, and "'all around Her, and beneath her light feet, causes the grass to grow.'"[42] We discover her traces all over the garden, such as the five-pointed star-shaped flowers and fruit, or the spirited, sensuously shaped petal forms, "the most beautiful sexual organs in the world,"[43] which often recall female genitals.

Beside the cherry and blackthorn blossoms, tulips open their ca-lyxes to reveal their phallic stamp, recalling Priapos, one of Aphrodite's and Dionysus's sons. He was a god of fertility revered in the shape of a large stone phallus. Thus, we also encounter male sexual forms at every turn in the garden.

Or small blue and white flowers, such as daisies, cat's eyes, bugles, and lady's smock, that turn a spring meadow into an enchanting bed. A lovers' bed perchance? A glimpse across the fence reveals our neighbor's barren, flowerless space – a perfect Swiss lawn. Oh, how dull and sad!

Glaringly red hibiscus blossoms are ablaze in summer (see next page). We associate these with a beautiful woman wearing them in her hair. They are so beautiful that we wish to preserve them forever! In fact, they bloom but for a day, and another, perhaps even more beautiful one, will open the next day. I suppose this might usher in some human wisdom. But let me move on, since we are about to discover, marvel at, and relish the beauty and sensuousness of the garden.

How about a short walk in the garden? I will refrain from describing anything beyond first-hand apperception. What is unforeseeable, though, is how my mood affects the perceived, and which stories and fantasies it will evoke before my mind's eye.

A morning in June: a light rain fell during the night and the garden is now transpiring with fragrance. Still standing at the garden gate, I can see the fat brown and blackish snails scuttling across the stone slabs. They seem like ships on the open sea, passing by slowly and silently – like sailing vessels. I appear to be in an affable mood, or else a less poetic notion of these nauseous things would occur to

me, whose sole objective is to eat my vegetables. I also catch sight of some Burgundy snails bearing their large, nice houses on their backs. How savvy to carry one's house on one's back; the sight of these snails strikes a chord with the Nomadic blood running through my veins and renders these creatures likable. I have always had a soft spot for these "housed" Burgundy snails on account of my former profession. Some years ago, I discovered that they were not as slow as they are said to be. At the time, I used to embellish all snails on the eastern side of the house with a pink dot of nail varnish, and those on the western side with dark-red. I was eager to discover how fast and whither they crawled. In effect, they made rapid progress and before long the pink dots commingled with the dark-red ones. Gimmickry in the garden, you might ask? Well, it invites such, too!

A large walnut tree comes into view. Up and up it grows, bursting with good health and beauty. Its nuts are starting to bud. The outer shells are still green, their forms small but plainly erotic. What's that, fantasies, already in the morning? But let us leave the walnut tree for now and cast our eye towards the raspberry and blackberry bushes growing beside it. They hold the promise of exciting views and tastes as well as delighting our sense of touch since there is something profoundly sensuous about picking soft, velvety raspberries. Raspberries stretch out towards us affectionately, awaiting our harvesting hands.

Blackberries behave quiet differently, protecting their fruit with long and thorny tendrils and leaves. "Let us be," they appear to be saying. Yet we do not let them be, but attempt to weave our fingers gingerly through the thorny entanglement to grasp the blackberries. I would never wear gloves to pick blackberries, since I would be spoiling the fun of exercising caution with the thorns. The berries should be picked slowly and appreciatively in August, turning them into creamy Blackberry jelly, the queen of all desserts. Perfect sensual pleasure unfolds before our eyes when the family is sitting at the table, each member drawing patterns in the dark violet fruit with liquid cream. Our eyes, noses, and palates relish the sight and taste, our hands guide the well shaped silver spoon, and our ears delight in the sound of others going into raptures.[44]

In June, this is but pleasant anticipation, but it was precisely this thrill that had prompted me to forget those prosaic matters, such as watering, dunging, and hoeing. I had already experienced so much on that June morning, without even stepping further into the garden. Now, however, I am sauntering along the small path. Darkgreen-reddish peppermint grows rampant on one side. It gives off an aromatic vapor, and I am pleased that it likes the none too fertile garden soil. Chives and of course parsley grow beside the peppermint. I like the latter in particular, since seeing it sprawl in the garden and chopping it in the kitchen forever remind me of the affable and ingenious Italian fairy tale, which we encountered in the previous chapter (see pages 81f.).

Parsley is a most interesting herb: on the one hand, it has always served as an aphrodiasic[45]; on the other, I recall my southern friends using its decoction as an abortifacient. I doubt whether parsley actually helped, for these matters also seemed to sort themselves out unless I am mistaken. But it was these properties, I believe, that prompted the Brothers Grimm to replace "vulgar" parsley with harmless Rapunzel.[46] Anyway, I quite like the green herb sitting harmlessly beside beautifully arranged dishes in restaurants, precisely because it is not that harmless. It depends on "how" and "how much," as the witch in the tower says. ...

There is a splendid rosemary bush growing beside dill, sage, lovage (yet another herb associated with love?), melissa, and thyme. It, too, is the subject of an Italian fairytale[47]; it appears that these small, aromatic, full-bodied herbs have always inspired the human body and imagination. Herbs do not necessarily belong in every garden: on the one hand, they are part and parcel of every medicine cupboard; on the other – whether fresh or dried – they are undoubtedly the garnish to every dish, together with countless spices from across the world. Herb plants afford us the opportunity to indulge in our culinary creativeness and practise refining our taste buds.

Yet another beguilingly fragrant herb grows beside the rosemary in a beautiful pot, which I have placed on a small pedestal of bricks to keep the ravenous snails at bay: basil. As its name (Greek *basileus* for "king") suggests, it is a regal plant, of Indian origin, and sacred, presumably because, on the one hand, it deters harmful insects, and on the other, because it has a beneficial effect on human digestion. Nowadays, basil is used widely in Mediterranean cuisine and enjoys great popularity. Besides its most pleasing scent and taste, it is also nice to look at. There is a healthy, lavish, and sensuous air to its leaves.

There is also a delightful fairy tale about basil, entitled the "Basil Girl."[48] It is an Oriental, slow moving story about the pleasures and pains of love between the "green" basil girl, furnished with much sensuality and motherly wit, and a noble yet sophisticated and unworldly young man. The tale sways back and forth, our protagonists fall in love, punish each other, take flight from one another, and yet their paths forever cross; ultimately, the young man is utterly ensnared by the basil girl's sensuous-erotic fragrance, and so "they lived happily ever after." It is a long story, easy to tell, while the lady of the house leisurely crushes the basil leaves to "pesto" [49] with a pestle and mortar.

On this June morning, there is not enough time to recount the tale of the basil girl. There is, however, a shorter account in Boccaccio's "Decameron,"[50] in which the healing power of basil plays an important role, but is unfortunately not strong enough to lead to a happy ending. The tale is somewhat sad and at variance with a chapter on the joy, beauty, and sensuousness of a garden. I would like to recount it nevertheless, since it reminds us how rapidly envy, jealously, and malice can destroy beauty and sensuousness, and joy in particular.

Couched in Boccaccio's distinctive, somewhat ribald language, this is the tale of a young woman whose brothers, driven by jealousy, batter to death their workmate, who is also their sister's sweetheart, and bury him a long way out of town. The young woman has no idea what has happened to her beloved. In her despair and misery, he appears to her in a dream and indicates the spot where he has been buried. She goes to the site and finds him, but she is unable to carry his whole body back home. She removes the head and buries it in her garden in a large pot in which she then plants basil.

Soon, the herb grows rampant, nurtured by love and watered by the young woman's tears. The prospering basil on the one hand, and the young woman's saddened eyes and waning beauty on the other, however, arouse her brothers' suspicion (or rather envy and malice), and they start digging up the soil surrounding the pot. They find the head and remove it once and for all. Unable to endure this loss, the young woman dies.[51]

The tale is so significant because the brothers not only slay their sister's sweetheart physically – she might have been able to overcome this loss and find another beloved – but they also kill her soulmate. Comprising both the young man's mind and soul, the flowerpot redoubles the garden motif; we can imagine it as the innermost alchemical vessel standing in the soul garden. Employing this vessel, she endeavors to transform and render fruitful her beloved's spirit and essence through her sorrowful tears. She succeeds in doing so, and interestingly a grief grows into that very plant – basil – conducive to digestion and metamorphosis. The young woman could have thus commuted and digested her beloved's spirit, thereby incorporating and rendering it fruitful within herself, had her brothers refrained from preventing this, too. What a thought-provoking tale!

As an alchemical vessel standing in the garden, the flowerpot recalls a coffin or urn resting in a small, private garden, the grave, and the larger communal garden, the cemetery. We attend to, sow plants in, and shed tears at a grave – where all those many memories, images, and feelings connecting us with a loved one or those close to us reside. Ever so slowly, these images and feelings change within us and become part of our own soul. Who is allowed to disturb or even impede this process?

As I emerge from beholding the basil pot standing in my garden on that June morning, Boccaccio's tale seems to me well worth considering in another sense: many women are familiar with such "brothers" as inner figures placed beside them within a family from an early age as part of a mindset averse to life and love. Such "inner brothers" foil their joy of life and thwart new momentum, impeding any love from entering the "family house" from outside and becoming fecund. Such an attitude towards love and life is diametrically opposed to

Aphrodite's spirit, the goddess of the garden and love. She loves softly vacillating movement, gentle ambulation, development, new connections – and not the violent, suffocating character of such "brothers."

Boccaccio's tale is sad and yet it contains an important element forming part of the garden, namely digestion, transformation, processing, and fertile reflowering. Innumerable small herbs at first grow in a garden, helping us digest difficult foods or matters upsetting our stomach. Such herbs are the garden's gifts to our blooming and health.

Yet the garden is itself a large vessel of change, in which seasonal change recurs on an annual basis, undergoing growth, bloom, fruition, withering, and decay, or digestion and reblooming. Such change proceeds gently in the garden, and there is something comforting and promising about it. It allows our confidence in the return of light and living growth to flourish. While the same rhythms and processes occur beyond the garden out in nature, we experience these much more intensely and immediately through our hands and hearts by tilling the soil within the personal, familiar space of our garden.

In the garden we come into very close physical and spiritual contact with seasonal changes: the soil and plants feel quite different in spring than they do in autumn, and we can literally touch the season with our hands. We can also sense ongoing change in our hearts. We rejoice at growth and blooming, whereas decay affords us a sense of sorrow and melancholy. We withstand silence in winter – perhaps we bridge the gap to spring through conjuring up a "spring carpet" – only to delight in the rebirth of life and happiness in spring when the first green leaves shoot out of the soil (see pages 19 and 22).

I once knew a small boy who would throw himself onto a field in spring and toss and turn on it as soon as the ground had become slightly warmer and the grass greener! We learn about these large secrets of natural life in the garden. We mirror ourselves in it, and it mirrors itself in us. It reflects tranquility and confidence in the natural processes of change – and of hope. Going for a walk in a garden is easily the best remedy against despondence, since we almost always discover something unexpected that raises a smile, affords pleasure, and raises hopes. You will have experienced this yourself without doubt.

I also dare claim that gardens mirror benevolence. Plants are not malicious, and neither are true gardeners. I have at least never come across a malicious gardener, neither in life nor in fairy tales and stories. On the contrary, gardeners are mostly quiet, helpful, and wise individuals, standing on firm ground and inspiring confidence. They are optimists, too, for their plans and notions of forthcoming beauty and joy tend to carry them somewhat ahead of time.

Gardens are also a source of great inspiration! It amuses me how much gardening books and leaflets fire my imagination. Even though I know perfectly well that my garden soil lacks the necessary constitution for magnificently porcelain blue larkspur to grow, it continues to enchant me. An inner voice says: "If only one flower would bloom in magnificent blue in a pot filled with the proper soil! Or failing that, at least one dressed in the most beautiful shades of blue? Or at least a painting all in blue." Revelling in blue ... and for the imagination to leap from blue to yellow. Perhaps an inspiration in sun colors? Or possibly plant the entire garden with sunflowers of every imaginable size? How about purple coneflowers, sunshine-like tagetes, or sun-yellow nasturtiums – my imagination revels in a sun-colored orgy!

Or an orgy of copper-gold-orange. After all, we are strolling through the garden on a June morning – so let us pause beside my most beloved rose bush! Thirty-eight rose plants grow in my garden, yet none is as aphrodisiacal as this particular specimen, ablaze in copper orange. Everything about it is fluid and soft, its twigs, flowers, softly curved petals, even its thorns are not painful. Its petals feel delicate and soft on the skin. Not like velvet or silk, but cool, almost moist, and yet they leave not a drop on our hands. When it rains, the fascicles bend downward softly; when the sun shines anew, the petals open again to reveal their golden yellow filaments. Its flower is neither simple nor fulsome, but soft and playful. It retains the unadulterated charm of wild roses, but cultivation has rendered it more incandescent and sophisticated.

This is a congenial mixture of nature and culture, which abstains from "overbreeding" the original beauty of wild flowers but emphasizes it more than ever. The color of this aphrodisiacal rose is a beautiful mixture, moreover, not only of fiery orange or copper tones, neither yellowish nor reddish, but a bit of everything contributes to its miraculous kaleidoscope. It eludes definition, appearing differently today than it does tomorrow, and varying in June and September. While its color remains indeterminate, its flower eschews coercion. It resists being cut and confined to a vase, for then it withers quickly. And yet one would like to decorate the entire house with this beguilingly fragrant rose. Its scent is not heavy and befuddling like that of dark red roses, but ethereal, tempting, erotic, flickering prankishly, and enshrouding us like Aphrodite's dancing veil.

The reader may have already guessed that this is the very rose of the goddess of love. Aphrodite, too, eludes entrapment and constraint, vacillating between the most delicate pink and fiery orange. Like my favorite rose, she, too, arouses our senses to indulge not in crude hedonism and fustian sensuality, but soft harmony situated between natural simplicity and cultivated, refined elegance. She teaches us the art of tempting yet non-stifling fragrance, lightfooted, agile grace, cheerful, non-malicious laughter, and pleasurable prankishness. Like my favorite rose, Aphrodite, too, has painful thorns, but even these can be exciting.

I wish to underline what else my rose and the goddess of love share: both require great affection and nourishment. Woe betide if they are neglected! They will run wild: the rose will lose its refined beauty and cultivated elegance and the goddess will turn into destructive, primitive hatred. In this condition, however, the rose is much more agreeable than the betrayed, offended goddess. For the latter merely returns to being a delicately blooming, plain wild rose. Roses may perhaps become sad, but never malicious and vindictive.

Let us reconsider the gifts that Venus-Aphrodite and the rose bestow on us: joy, beauty, and sensuality. These are most valuable gifts, to which we should afford much space and affectionate devotion in return. Beauty and joy are divine sparks, rendering life worth living.

Our senses are the gates to the world, our fellow humans, and our own souls. Would it not be worthwhile to open these gates? We ought to foster such sensuality, just as we cultivate nature in our gardens.

Let us return to Venus and the garden once again. In *Gods and Planets*, Ellynor Barz observes: "Astrology associates Venus with conviviality, enjoyment, aesthetics, indulgence, luxury, lust; with art, beauty, play, and sensuality; with a sense of proportion and harmony; with striving for balance and complement, harmony and well-being."[52] Is she referring to Venus? Or gardens? I will leave you to decide for yourself!

Let us continue our morning walk a bit further: past lavish, fragrant roses, past blooming bushes and magnificent flowers, over to the pots containing seedlings. In spring, I had sown petunias in small bowls. Later, I pricked and repotted them in larger pots. Doing so afforded me pleasure, and it was a task replete with hope and the anticipation of innumerable medium-blue, deep-blue and white fragrant blooms. The garden seduces us to entertain a certain greed for even more flowers, even more beautiful variants. We would surely become insatiable if such mundane issues as time, money, and – a garden fence, precisely, did not curb our "intoxication with plants." Our desire for more and more beauty is forever "cut back."

Now, however, I relish the prospect of many healthy plants and repot them once more, grouping them and using larger pots. I cannot explain what makes burrowing and digging in the soil so soothing and satisfying. Perhaps you have managed to answer this question for yourself. It strikes me as one of our primordial activities, associated with survival and the continuation of life, although primarily with any other creative activity capable of evoking a profound feeling of happiness. Something else comes into play in the flower garden: nothing obliges us to plant flowers, for we could survive without them. But we are allowed to – and to our heart's delight, moreover!

Let us consider a small, nicely shaped clay pot in which I have planted memories, small fragrant memories that continue to afford me great joy. I behold the small pot containing the small carnations.

Images arise and blend with the scent of childhood. A small, wistful tear over the lost paradise drops into the pot. Thankfully, I have no "malicious brothers" seizing my memories like the young woman's in Boccaccio's tale! – Is that not a titmouse chirping in the apple tree? Memories can shuttle back and forth between my grandfather's breakfast table and my apple tree. They can weave threads between the past and present. Can they also fly into the future? Indeed they can, for the apple tree no longer belongs to me alone, but has grown to tell a story for my grandchildren. I wonder whether they will one day recall their grandmother's glowing red apples?

Chapter Six

Love's Garden: Another Secret Place

It would seem that world literature abounds with more descriptions, poems, and songs about gardens of love than of any other habitat. From the magical, fairytale gardens of "Arabian Nights,"[53] where lovers meet secretly, to Giorgio Bassano's stirring "The Garden of the Finzi-Continis"[54] and its account of the budding love between two young people and their forays among old, walled gardens, to the affectionate tale of the "Secret Garden,"[55] a small, enchanted garden in which two children experience joy, love, and well-being, gardens, have always represented a sheltered space replete with beauty, sensuousness, and fertility, where the secret of love between two people can unfold.

Some of the gardens of love that are described and sung about actually exist, but most, including those mentioned above, are neither tangible nor accessible. Yet they are part of reality and continue to delight and invigorate our imagination. Perhaps you recall a garden bench or an enchanted path between radiant flowers and shady bushes where a small romance loomed between yourself and someone you were really fond of? Of course you do! While that romantic encounter is possibly long past, the scent, the play of light and shade, the secret and enchantment of the garden have struck root in your heart.

Let us accept the invitation of an unknown poet to enter the garden of his soul. We, too, are addressed, as much as the unknown beloved for whom he wrote these lines. Let him guide us into his soul and seduce us to roam around our own inner gardens.

The Key

I wish to open the door
Of the gardens of my soul to you.

So that we may both enjoy
The flowers and butterflies
In their array of colors.

So that we may both enjoy
The back and forth/volleying of the birds
And their songs early and late.

So that we may both enjoy
The play of the wind
As it delicately sways our plants,
large and small,
And caresses our hair
And skin.

So that we may both enjoy
The bright sunlight
And feel its warmth soak into our bodies,
Two as one in sunwarm coalescence.

So that we both enjoy
The taste of ripe fruit
Melting sweetly on our lips.

May you welcome the moon
In my garden with the morning and evening star
And experience this glimpse of the night,
The nightingale's song,
The gentle nightwind
And the moonlight,
The perfume of petals at night,
Garnet scent and berries.

I want you to enter my garden.
Here is the key.
Please come.

So let us take the key and enter! The poet is a person blessed with ample inner wealth, for he possesses not merely *one* garden but many *gardens* of the soul. Moreover, he is generous, trustworthy, and loving. Or how else could he grant another person such unimpeded access to his inner realm?

"I wish to open the door
Of the gardens of my soul to you."

The opening two lines already open the gate to a vast world. Borne by our imagination, we enter a vast space ablaze with green and a myriad of colors, paths, grounds, tree tops, undergrowth, briar woods, ponds, and meadows covered in flowers. We discover gardens of joy and desire, melancholy and sorrow. They are silent, turned inward. Perhaps dead and withered loves were buried beneath weeping willows. We then discover a rampant, colorful garden of sensuality and eroticism – plainly evident in the poem – but probably also a concealed fencing garden, ready for aggression, combat, and contest. There is certainly a small god's garden in which a solitary flower stands abloom, one which unites everything, including a hop garden and arbor, a vegetable garden, a poet's garden, a stalactite cave for rage, grievance, and thoughts of retreat, a witch's garden containing innumerable healing and poisonous herbs, and ones capable of confusing the senses. We can imagine all of this.

The poet opens many gardens of human existence to another being and us, and these spaces come alive in a myriad of lights and shadows, shining colors, shades and obscurities, recounting emotions and the diversity of human life. Our imagination celebrates a feast and expands infinitely. It grows boundless, able to fathom all heights and depths. It can also discover the realms of the abysmal and destruction.

The poet's imagination, however, does not probe that far in this poem. Rather, he opens up the prankish and erotic spiritual spheres of togetherness and sensuality. His intention is not to show us the dark caverns of our spiritual garden. This would frighten his beloved and deter her from entering. Love almost always tempts us with charming images, ensnares us with the colorful veil of illusion, as gardens do with their flowers and scents. And once we are entrapped, those tedious everyday chores, such as weeding and being mindful of thorns, begin.

Let us pursue the poet's enticing images. He wishes to relish the sunshine with his beloved, and yet he also wants her to welcome the gentle moon and Venus, the morning and evening star, and to enshroud herself in its enchanting light. His garden appears somewhat fabulous, replete with magic and charm.

And thus my mind's eye conjures up a round garden in which human and elves — the latter are creatures mostly only beheld with the mind's eye — are dancing together. They are dancing around a fountain, whose jet of water shoots upwards and tumbles downwards playfully and effervescently. Fountains belong to all gardens as open hearths to houses. Fire and water are the central elements bestowing life on a house and garden. Originally, houses were constructed as sheltered spaces to protect the precious, holy fire[56]; the very first gardens in human history were oases that existed, greened, and bloomed on account of a spring. The fountain confers upon the garden fertility and life, which accounts for the fact that a woman's private, moist parts are often referred to as a "garden."

Yes, humans and elves are dancing round the fountain of love in the garden. It could also be that love is dancing its own dance, sometimes gently and appreciatively, sometimes wildly and passionately; at times we see her, at times she is veiled .... Love is a dance with the veil!

Quite rightly so, the cynics will remark: "Initially, the veil is pink and flaps lustfully in the wind — soon it hangs there dark grey, torn asunder by thorns, affording an image of neverending horror." Unfortunately, cynics cling to a one-sided view of the world; in particular, they disbelieve that Venus's treasure chest contains many different veils:

shortlived ones prone to easily tear, but also more robust ones possessing the magical property to forever renew themselves.

Almost everyone has known or suspected for centuries that the veil belongs to Venus-Aphrodite; many images and paintings bear witness to this affectionate couple, Venus and the veil. Both the latter, this delicate robe wafting in the wind, and movement and dance – they all play for lover and lovers. Is it not thus: sometimes we behold our beloved through a pink veil, sometimes through a grey and nebulous shroud, and then not at all, since the veil covers everything; sometimes the veil is resolutely cast to one side, and we behold our counterpart with compelling, unveiled clarity?

Is this horrifying? Sobering? Clarifying? Soothing? Does such a realistic view afford us brief rays of hope or permanent deterrence? Probably both. Be that as it may – what makes the human being singular is that such insight, that is, beholding what lies behind the veil, is mostly brief. No more than a gust of wind is required to inflate the veil anew; it recommences its prankishness and resumes its dance.

It is often good thus, since the veil mercifully conceals what should not be seen, such as deepest sorrow or abject horror. Alas, great moments of happiness are concealed, too!

Often, swiftly lowering a veil is not good either, since a clear view is all too readily obscured. Yet who can judge what is either good or bad in the here and now? For it is not we who move the veil. It is the wind that "blows from where it wishes" – and it, too, is a "celestial child." Phrased somewhat differently, there is a far greater power than our ego consciousness raising and lowering the veil. Upon close and patient observation of our own life, we can recognize this interplay between our consciousness and that which remains unconscious and concealed. Sometimes the veil rises, sometimes it conceals, forever in its own good time.

The dance continues: I see you, you see me not; we behold each other, no one should see us! Search for me – no, don't follow me! Does the dance not recall a young children's game? They grab hold of a small cloth, a colored ribbon, or their mother's dress, and play: "Where am I? Here I am!" And they play with the cloth exactly as they would with a veil, as yet somewhat clumsily, but very coquettishly and prankishly. Small Venuses and love-birds. And they can roar with laughter doing so, a pleasurable laughter when the veil is drawn and mother and child once again behold each other!

We used to relish another game in our grandparents' garden, albeit one played without a veil. It, too, was a dance of sorts – of happening upon or rather eluding one another. We called it "Got-you." We would eagerly stomp up and down the gravel paths between the flower beds surrounded by box hedges. What mattered most was that we did *not* happen upon one another. "I've got you." – "No, you haven't!" "Oh yes, I have!" – "Oh no, you haven't!" It was a simple yet amusing game, perfectly suited to a somewhat old-fashioned garden in which someone took the time to cut the box hedges and rake the gravel paths. But it also consisted of a dance involving two partners ostensibly reluctant to encounter one another, but actually very intent on finding each other. It was a small, harmless game at the time. Playing always involves surprises; they teach us to both accept the unexpected and become flexible. They instruct us to commute between different worlds.

But let us cast a veil over this children's pastime and return to the poem. The poet also has a romantic soul, and we could imagine him strewing rose petals on his beloved's bed. His repetition of the words "may we both rejoice" suggests that he attaches great importance to togetherness. He desires common endeavor and mutual experience in his soul garden.

Lovers have always longed to share sight, hearing, smell, touch, and enterprise. Eating together is a particularly intimate affair, closely associated with sexual union by indigenous peoples. Yet "sleeping together" renders explicit the most intimate sphere of togetherness: this everyday phrase for sexual union expresses the dissolution of self-involved consciousness and the intoxicating fusion of two individuals, akin to the dissolved, very narrow, and yet highly spacious consciousness experienced in sleep.

The connection between two people sleeping side by side goes much further in that they enter into association in the depths of the unconscious. We should probably sleep only beside those we trust, just as we should invite only those trusted persons into our spiritual garden.

Dreams and sleep, the inner and outer gardens, and the goddess's veil are linked: she forms the mysterious "realm in-between," that very particular spiritual realm between human consciousness and the complete other, be this an utterly different individual, the deep unconscious of the night, or entirely unknown nature beyond the garden.

Is the in-between world of our dreams not situated in our soul garden, between our everyday individual consciousness and the dark, alien, impersonal unconscious? Does not one dream superimpose itself on another like an intangible, often nebulous veil? At times, dreams are more comprehensible because they are colored more by waking consciousness; at other times, they are truly "incomprehensible" and bring us into contact with mystery and the enigmas of the remote, greater unconscious.

Depending on the coloring of the dream veil, images appear in superimposed layers, the various emotional charges of the veil thicken, and ultimately a meaningful connection emerges. But the dreams

remain veil layers forever, for one can never say: "Now I have fully grasped the meaning!" The veils shift continuously: one rises, another superimposes itself thereupon – in a neverending dance of veils, a ceaseless dance of dreams in the soul garden. At times we believe we have understood a dream, only for it to withdraw again. Feeling our way into dreams, and interpreting them, requires incredible agility, for we must forever pursue the playful, dancing movements of our soul.

Dancing with one's garden is equally animated and ever changing. The garden changes hourly through the vicissitudes of light, wind, temperature, and seasonal change. It blooms vigorously in spring and summer, causing us to marvel. The grass appears to be growing before our eyes while new flowers bloom and others wither almost hourly. The colors of flowers become ever more intense and the leaves increasingly greener until they shift toward luminous yellow and red in autumn.

Then the leaves fall, and countless veils – cobwebs – traverse the garden (see following page).

They exist – they are visible, and yet they are not – for they are beyond grasp. Might these be the sisters of our dreams? They, too, span the space between our consciousness and the increasingly blurred background. Or do they perhaps catch our dreams? Native Americans call the ornate cobweb-like forms that they hang above their beds to catch bad dreams "dream catchers."[57] Dreams and cobwebs are certainly daughters of the great weaver weaving the pattern of our destiny. But notice that both the spider's web and our dreams, the garden and love, can ensnare us! We can get carried away and become embroiled, losing our footing.

Everyday moods are often "veiled," too! Feelings of love, however, are the most mysterious and erratic. Love is up in the air one minute and down the next, oscillating between childlike, sweet pink, passionate red, and deep, fragrant, velvet purple akin to the sounds of a sonorous cello. Love dances like flowers in the wind, butterflies hovering over flowers, and sometimes like stars high above the garden at night. It can be as deadly as a frosty night, as venomous and confusing as belladonna, as engulfing as winds in the garden or as unwavering as grass that keeps growing again to form safe ground.

We discover a myriad of connections between love and the garden. In particular in the Middle Ages, gardens not only symbolized the beloved but also (courtly) love itself. Various subtle and oblique images, such "flowerpicking" and "defloration," alluded to highly intimate experience; others, such as "the pleasurable spice garden" or "rose garden," epitomized the most exalted bliss of love and its raptures.[58] The "harmless" images of the garden willingly lend themselves to describing less harmless appetites and events. The nasty experiences that occur to us in the garden are apposite expressions of hurt feelings.

There can be no doubt, however, that a blooming, fragrant, fecund garden arouses human sensuality and the body to the highest. Our soul, too, becomes susceptible, soft, and attuned to exchanging feelings.

And thus a most particular connection arises between two individuals strolling through gardens. They can speak figuratively and couch their feelings and desires in the enchanting images of nature.

Feelings of love often become possible only in the sheltered space afforded them by a garden. Our feelings need images to which we can attach them. They require comparisons, circumlocutions, images of color and scent, and gestures. Our souls and bodies know what love means.

Imparting these feelings to someone else calls for translation into images, sounds, smells, words capable of illustration; or we can resort to dancing and physical expression. Somehow we must all proffer our feelings to others. The opulent vitality of the garden as such provides a wealth of opportunities, ranging from "the red roses one gives to a beautiful woman" to the small, old-fashioned adage often found in albums: "Roses, tulips, carnations / all three wither / only one does not / forget-me-not."

It seems to me that we have not yet unravelled the true meaning of gardens for lovers. In what follows, I wish to impart my own notion of this mystery.

Love is very probably among the most difficult and beautiful matters of human existence. It spans utmost happiness and deepest pain. It can be like a ray of light reaching earth or an unexpected angel attempting to alight beside us. Yet who instructs their children how to deal with love? Who prepares their souls for this experience that changes everything?

Love's ray of light is a piercing, heartwarming, yet also merciless gift. It can set a soul garden abloom in a miraculous manner. In everyday parlance, we also speak of love as a "bolt out of the blue," striking like lightning. Such a bolt is even more merciless, no longer experienced as a gift but as an overpowering force, wreaking havoc on those whose souls are unprepared.

The angel in turn is also a gift, albeit a delicate, fragile, and vulnerable one. The angel of love would like to be received, accepted, and cherished. The angel needs protection and food, available in the well-tended, cultivated soul garden finely attuned to subtle oscillations. Settling in a neglected, parched garden proves difficult for the angel, since he is hardly recognized as an angel of love, but finds himself mistaken for clumsy, heavy-footed beings that have ravaged the child's soul garden early on. The angel needs an appreciative, animated, and strong soul to gain a foothold and flourish. The soul is the nurturing, protective vessel wherein love is transformed and refined and can grow and bear fruit.

Thus we return to the image of the garden, gardening, all the effort and responsibility that cultivating the inner and outer garden demands as well as the joy and happiness arising therefrom. I attach great importance to paying utmost heed to the vigor, vitality, receptiveness, and power of resistance of our soul garden and our children's so that gardens may also become gardens of love.

In the sheltered vessel of the soul garden, the angel of love can settle and become effective. He fecundates the garden, and it enriches him in return. The soul garden bestows upon him its entire wealth of subtle, cultivated feelings, its manifold beauty, and its fervent, intense vitality so that his wings spread in delight. He begins to dance and sing, and soon attracts others to draw close. He opens the garden to the gardens of the soul and invites them to enter. The dance begins. We accompany the dancers with the first stanza of a song for Hathor, the ancient Egyptian goddess of joy, song, dance, love, and fertility:

> "Come, golden one, whom song sustains,
> Whose heart longs to dance,
> Who shines with jubilation in times of rest,
> Who loves to dance in the dark."[59]

Chapter Seven

Stillness: The Experience of the Divine in Gardens

It is Sunday morning in a sprawling English park. Magnificent trees spread their branches and stand tall like ancient, wise figures seeking to protect the peace and quiet in the park. The grass at the foot of the trees is soft and sways gently in the lazy morning wind. We leave the driveway and walk across the grass to a small chapel. It stands there affably and somewhat quaint between the trees. Roses grow from its yellowish walls. A particularly beautiful pink and orange colored type climbs the wall and entwines a small window. Its sweet scent reminds me that only English roses smell like this.

At the chapel entrance I am handed a small red prayer book and a Bible. Only then do I catch sight of the interior. Its beauty enchants me. Everything inside the chapel is red: the prayer books, the long carpet leading down the aisle to the altar, the clergyman's cassock, and the small embroidered cushions, bearing different motifs, on which we will later kneel. I choose one with flowers in my desire to kneel on a small garden.

White flowers, arranged in numerous lavish, romantic bouquets, suffuse the chapel. Small and large ones, white carnations, jasmine twines, large white roses, and in particular charming small white roses dangling down in dainty clusters. The flowers have been set into ample green, rampant foliage – loosely and naturally, unlike the stiff arrangements so common in churches and chapels elsewhere in Europe. The green foliage resembles a green veil throwing into relief

120

the beauty and purity of the white flowers. I am deeply moved by the flower arrangements. These radiate such delicate femininity that I assume they could only have been furnished for a most extraordinary and very feminine woman.[60]

I am not less moved by the altar cloth, albeit quite differently. It, too, is green – a soft and salubrious green. It is the same green as the fields surrounding the chapel, and as the leaves in the bouquets inside the chapel. The cloth covers the entire chapel altar and hangs down the front to the floor. The green is embroidered with gold. A golden mandorla-shaped corona surrounds the green area at the center of the cloth. A golden tree, the tree of life, has been embroidered on this central area. To the left and right of the mandorla, the corona passes over into horizontal rays spread out like arms and hands seeking to impart the message of the golden tree of life standing in green nature. The same motif has been embroidered on the ends of the green stole that the clergyman is wearing over his red gown.

We attend a short mass, without a sermon, but with many jointly spoken prayers. We partake in the Lord's Supper at the green-golden altar. We leave the small chapel, and the experience of the service in the charming, sacral atmosphere of the interior of the chapel flows out into the expansive park. The park, a castle garden, accepts our human feelings of awe and gratitude towards the creation and returns these with the existence of the trees, fields and hedges, flowers and ponds. A dialogue between nature and humankind ensues, an exchange of vibrations and the inner knowledge of togetherness, and that both are made of the same matter and part of the same creation. Just as God spoke to us in the chapel and we answered him in our heart and through our prayers and song, he spoke to us about the life of the trees and fields, and we answered him with our awe and love of creation.

Most people have probably experienced this sense of being one with nature or the universe that we mostly experience as the starlit sky overhead. It is a primordial sense of what the contemporary physicist and mystic Brian Swimme articulates in his *The Universe is a Green Dragon*[61] when Thomas, the older, more experienced man, instructs

Kim, his younger counterpart: "Most amazing is this realization that everything that exists in the universe came from a common origin. The material of your body and the material of my body are intrinsically related because they emerged from and are caught up in a single energetic event. Our ancestry stretches back through the life forms and into the stars, back to the beginnings of the primeval fireball. This universe is a single multiform energetic unfolding of matter, mind, intelligence, and life. And all of this is new. None of the great figures of human history were aware of this. Not Plato, or Aristotle, or the Hebrew Prophets, or Confucius, or Thomas Aquinas, or Leibniz, or Newton, or any other world-maker. We are the first generation to live with an empirical view of the origin of the universe. We are the first humans to look into the night sky and see the birth of stars, the birth of galaxies, the birth of the cosmos as a whole. Our future as a species will be forged within this new story of the world."[62]

Brian Swimme is probably right to observe that while humanity lacks exact knowledge of such relations, we have always had some notion and an inner certainty about being one with the universe if we only cared to listen or look deeply enough into our own depths.

Listening and looking into ourselves requires space, time, and silence. The commotion in the streets, the forever changing tunes on the wireless, flickering television images, the frenetic pace of everyday life all impede turning towards the soul. They disturb and destroy the primordial space, the void, "nothingness" in which nothing other than nature's most subtle primordial music resides, in which something new and significant can emerge, assume shape, and evolve.

Silence in the garden, silence in the soul, silence in the garden of the soul. There only the gentle vibrations of the cosmos are audible, permitting the human soul to enter into the transient oscillation of the primordial music of the world. Let us enter our garden, either the tangible or imaginary one. Let us sit down on a small stone bench or the grass. Let us listen to the garden's soft sounds.

Initially, we perceive only some very few: a delicate singing in the air, rustling in the arid leaves, birdsong, the wind in the trees, the chortling of

a small stream. Let us listen more closely, let us harken. Not only one bird is singing, but many different ones rendering themselves audible in their own language. We also hear bees humming in the flowers, the metallic sound of a large dragonfly's wings, and the unmistakable call of a kite flying over the garden.

The wind, too, emits many different sounds: the arid, somewhat sharp rustling of bamboo leaves, the regular, deep swooshing of the great oak, and the slender, hardly audible sounds emerging from the drooping vines. We can distinguish the many different sounds of the leaves dancing in the wind. Only the small stream chortles and chuggles away evenly. We also hear ourselves, our breathing, our heart beat; we are part of the larger whole. Yet we not only hear a symphony of sounds, we also pick up various scents. We smell the water nearby, the grass, earth, and flowers. Perhaps we can even smell the wind. I think I can smell the wind.

We behold a myriad of different shapes in the leaves, flowers, bushes, and trees. We can play with these shapes. We can see that which we already know, bushes and flowers that have been forever. But we can also catch sight of the hitherto unknown. Forms can be separated and reassembled in larger, hitherto unknown formations. It is a neverending game.

Colors also come into view, in particular an incredible number of different shades of grey. They serve as a background in the garden, forming a backdrop, so to speak, for the luminescent shades of red, orange, and yellow, the deep, velvet-like shades of blue and violet, or the light, mellow pastel-colored flowers. Its contrast with the various shades of grey brings each color to life.

Nature conjures into existence a miraculous kaleidoscope of different greens. We are usually only ever aware of this play of greens if we attend to it consciously. While green is perhaps normally described as soothing, it is often said to be commonplace and even boring. And yet green is the color of hope, growth, life, and even resurrection. It is the elementary force and primordial color of life, surrounding us in the garden unless we are engulfed by the height of winter.

Green is probably the color that best relaxes our eyes, exhausted from gazing at a computer screen; it also invigorates tired minds, and imbues the sick with energy and hope. Once again (as intimated in Chapter 3), I feel prisoners should not be deprived of at least a glimpse of nature.

Let us dwell somewhat longer on the color green, which I have termed the primordial color of life, but which is in actual fact no primary color like red, blue, or yellow, but a blended color comprising blue and yellow. Green is a mediating color, the bridge between heaven and earth, sunlight and water. Green would thus be the color in-between, which allows the garden, the "mysterious space between" to become the greening sphere (see next page) of life and fertility. Green is the sacred color in all countries in which plant life is under constant threat from the arid desert, that is, where there is too much sun and not enough water.

According to the twelfth-century mystic Hildegard von Bingen, many contemporary scholars, and ordinary "insightful" individuals, green is the *sancta viriditas*, the "sacred force of greening" that pervades the macrocosm and microcosm of the human body as a "force from eternity." In her study of Hildegard von Bingen, [63] Ingrid Riedel observes: "What I find so appealing about her [Hildegard] is that she combines what was often severed in the history of Christianity. She is said to be a saint, and yet she bears the hallmark of all 'witches,' that is, of women said to be witches. She is revered at once as a saint and a great healer, possessing medical knowledge like those wise, early Celtic and Germanic female herbalists. Hildegard is a prophet – like Deborah, the great woman of the Old Testament. Her words provided counsel to leaders in her own time, including the emperor Frederick Barbarossa and several popes.

Hildegard was – and perhaps this defines her originality – both a healer and scientist. She knew more about plants and animals than anyone else in her time. What distinguishes her concept of nature is that a consistent life-giving force, the *sancta viriditas* or "sacred force of greening," pervades the entire macrocosm and microcosm.

This force inheres in the living plant as well as in the human body and not least in the human soul:

O noblest greenness,
rooted in the sun
and radiating joy
in the round of a circling wheel
uncontained by earthly splendor:
held by the heart force of divine mystery
you blush like daybreak
and flare with solar ardor.
Green, thou art
held close by love.

This green is thus 'the heart force of divine mystery' that is 'uncontained by earthly splendor.' As a force begotten of God, and bearing witness to him, it also becomes effective in all green matter in a figurative sense, such as in the union of man and woman. It assumes particular strength as a germinating force in the nascent child. It awakens nature in spring, and renders all growth mature." [64]

The same thoughts that Hildegard von Bingen captured in words eight centuries ago also permeate Brian Swimme, the modern physicist. The first chapter of his above-mentioned book bears the title "Reading the meaning in the cosmic story" and the subtitle "Creativity: Primordial and Pervasive." At the very beginning of the chapter, Kim, the younger, queries Thomas, the elder: *"But why say it's a green dragon when it obviously isn't?"* Thomas responds: "I call the universe a green dragon because I want to avoid lulling you into thinking we can have the universe in our grasp, like a stray dog shut up in its kennel. I want to remind us of this proper relationship as we approach the Whole of Things." [65]

Observing the symbolism of the dragon reveals that the "green dragon" aptly captures the creativeness of the universe. The dragon is a very old image for the tremendous elementary creative and destructive powers of the universe. A green dragon relates to Hildegard's sacred, creative green power, and represents the primordial form of growth, fertility, and life – that creative force affecting the entire evolution of the universe, earth, and humanity. It relates to the unfathomable secrets of life. [66]

In *What is Life?*, Lynn Margulis inquires into the nature, origin, and development of life, this eternal secret, through an investigation of four billion years of evolution. [67] The chapter entitled "The Transmutation of Sunlight" bears the small subtitle "Green Fire." At the end of this chapter, Margulis reiterates her basic question: *"So, what is life?"* In response, she writes: "Life is the transmutation of sunlight. It is the energy and matter of the sun become the green fire of photosynthesizing beings. It is the warmth of the tiger stalking the jungle in the dead of night. Green fire converts wildly to the red and orange and yellow and purple sexual fire of flowering plants. Expanding, developing lignin, green beings raised up the biosphere and spread it horizontally. As fossils these beings trapped the original gold of the sun, stocking wealth only recently released in the human crucible of the solar economy.

But the arrow in all these transformations must eventually become a loop that encloses the autopoietic exigencies of plants.[68] We may be an intelligent life form but our very intelligence depends on that part of us we now recognize as photosynthetic. As life transmutes solar fire into all the energy and matter cycles of the biosphere, we pay homage to the ingenious ascension of the living plant."[69]

It appears as if Lynn Margulis and Hildegard von Bingen are spiritually akin, too. Although Margulis never utters the word God, a deep reverence for the nature of life and astonishment at the creativeness of nature runs through what is a work of science. One senses that her scientific work probably made her even more profoundly aware of the existence of a divine creative force.

I would argue that we can only ever approach the essence of the "other" – be this the great natural world or an individual plant, a work of art or an everyday matter, or our own elusive nature – through longstanding, painstaking, and profound devotion. Through such religious preoccupation with ourselves or others, we inevitably come into contact with the wisdom of creation. Through the essence or soul of the other, and through a view of our own soul, we recognize the "complete Other" – God.

And thus it is in the garden: in turning at once completely outward – towards surrounding nature and culture (the garden, after all, connects both) and inward – towards our own essence, our own soul garden, we sense the unity of the inward and outward.

The stillness in the garden opens up a space in which we can experience an affinity between ourselves, as small individual beings, and both nature and the universe. We no longer feel alone, but part of a whole. We can smile (in the sense of feeling relaxed, happy, and peaceful) and say that we feel as secure in the sheltering garden as in the bosom of Mother Nature. Presumably, it is this sense of security experienced in the comprehensible green space that induces us, no matter how small or how old, to plant a garden.

Let us return to the stone bench in our garden. Or rather, let us now sit on the lawn, amid the "green power." Let us listen, smell, touch, and observe the garden once more – all its trees, flowers, bushes, soil, the small river, fountain, animals, birds, and butterflies. Let us feel ourselves, for we are part of all this. Let us become absorbed in the secret of the green fire, of the "green dragon," and of the "sacred force of greening." What is life? Which great creative force are we part of? These question ensue from observing – and being at one with – the garden; and it could be that they lead us to the secret we call God.

Chapter Eight

The Everyday: Gardening as Inner Work

Daily garden routine, as anyone tending a garden knows, spells not only joy, beauty, sensuousness, or silent meditation, but also many commonplace, arduous, and often tedious chores. We undertake these to keep order. Pursuing this aim could be compared to the innumerable and arduous small steps involved in climbing a mountain peak to indulge in the view.

Gardening involves a spate of moderately interesting tasks, such as mowing the lawn, weeding, gathering withered leaves. In return for such scarcely inspiring chores, we become unexpectedly oblivious of the heartache or annoyance that afflicted us beforehand. Or we cut the hedges and bushes, considering that we might do away with outworn habits to make room for new (spiritual) life. We might even become aware of the fact that we fertilize and water our plants, or attend to our flowers and vegetables more affectionately, than we do ourselves. It is true, is it not, that we often pamper our flowers, speak to them fondly, even yearn for them as we do for those we treasure while neglecting body and soul. Occasionally, we treat the garden much the same as people. We look after the plants we like with utmost devotion – and allow those to wither that contravene our worldview. Our dealings with our garden obviously mirror our character traits.

Countless connections exist between humankind and gardens, for both are living creatures that can be loved or despised, cherished or destroyed. Gardeners and gardens are involved in highly emotional, on occasion even emotionally charged relationships, comparable to

those between two individuals or between us and our own spiritual world.

There is a variegated exchange of forces between humankind and gardens, an ongoing give-and-take, and what is often a trial of strength or even struggle. Ultimately, this is to our benefit, it seems, or else we would hardly spend our lives toiling away in a garden (some would speak of marriage). Obviously, there are gardeners who worry themselves sick over the gardens, but I will abstain from dwelling on such characters, for self-torture is utterly alien to Aphrodite's nature, the goddess of the garden.

I would, however, like to recount a very particular experience that you undoubtedly share. Possibly our experiences are quite similar, since you, too, were chased through the highs and lows of your emotional world, either ending up exhausted or resigning to saying: "Well, I suppose there is no other alternative than to set to work ...."

Imagine a July morning. Your garden is ablaze (now, that's a slip of the pen, as I meant to write "abloom") and has never been as beautiful as this. We believe this every time we behold its splendor because we have forgotten the day before yesterday when we were tempted to embrace it for being so beautiful! The last roses linger while the first summer flowers shine brightly; Alfonso, the amicable gardener, has done a fine job trimming the grass; the potted blue petunias are a sheer delight; we relish the sight of the basil; and the weeds have not yet grown rampant – so it is about the worst time to leave the garden for a holiday.

And yet this is inevitable. We have made arrangements and cannot take our garden along like our dog, that loving companion. Nor can we entrust the garden to our kindhearted grandmother, as we might do with our children. So we find a reliable, adept individual to water our garden, neither too much nor too little, but with feeling. We cannot rely on the heavens, for we will discover that they cannot be relied on. Such "angels," who water other people's gardens and pots, exist – precisely because there are so many of us who cannot bear the sight of flowers or vegetables dying of thirst.

I, too, have found a loving "gardener" for the holiday season. And thus I prepare watering cans and hose pipes; I remove the snail bait since my proxy might object – either for the hedge-hogs' sake or because she has not grown the petunias (and is hence not inclined to dote on them with fanatical motherly love); I tie back the sunflower, snip a tendril to afford the grapes more force, place more fertilizer in the datura's soil to be on the safe side since it

has been quite meager this year; I cajole my garden into being good, and then leave.

While on holiday, I often think of my garden. Admittedly, not as often as I think of my family, but nonetheless. I wonder whether the heavens have collaborated with my "garden angel" to douse my flowers and vegetables with rain at night or whether they have plotted to swamp it with fierce hailstorms. Hail drills holes into the delicate petals, destroying their fruit and inflicting grief on every gardener's heart.

In foreign countries, I peep into foreign gardens, become envious at the sight of southern blossoms, and yearn for a warmer climate back home. These lavish bushes full of hibiscus flowers! How marvelous! How pathetic my potted hibiscus is by comparison! As mentioned, gardens fill us with longing, and we yearn for ever greater beauty and abundance. That said, the few blooms of my hibiscus plant are truly gorgeous! Can I never be content? I take myself to task for my insatiable appetite for flowers while knowing that it is my soul garden that lacks satisfaction. Bushes abloom with shining red hibiscus spell sun, light, warmth, joy, vigor, everything someone born in winter will always yearn for. Notwithstanding my insatiability, I very much love my garden, as I noted at the beginning of this book, and always return home with expectant joy. As I do on this occasion.

No sooner have I entered the house than I drop everything – my suitcase, handbag, exciting? letters – and rush out into the garden. How has it fared? How has it done without me? Is the magnificent, deep blue-violet Clematis still abloom? Are there any small tomatoes left? What about my sunflowers? This year I planted them in large clay pots to prevent the snails from chewing them up. I greet my garden like a child returning home to claim all its toys. Nothing has withered, everything is green and lush. Oh, thank you, dear garden angel! I relish the sight of the lush green abounding in my garden! Still well-disposed, I forgive the tomatoes for not bursting with fruit; I can buy tomatoes after all. But there *is* homegrown basil!

Now what has become of this herb, whose luscious, sensuous beauty and energy I used to praise? I discover some chewed-off stems in a pot whilst another contains some plants that I had providently placed on a pedestal out of reach. Poor, nibbled plants, not even enough for a thimbleful of pesto. These god____ snails; I condemn them at will, foulmouthing to myself, for they have obviously not only indulged in the basil but also nibbled at the petunias, and the tagetes bear mucilagnious traces. Had I only strewn snail baits around my loved ones – never mind nature conservation! Today, snails incite aggression and rather cruel fantasies in me.

For the moment, however, I suppress these malicious thoughts and even attempt to make the most of this grievance: the razored basil pot is now free for new plants. And I dare say that there is hardly anything more beautiful than empty space, empty sheets of paper, empty pots, unplanted patches of soil – for these all inspire the human imagination. How could the space be furnished? What could one write or draw on the paper? What else could I sow here? Or plant in that pot?

Presumably you are familiar with this little game. Sometimes we need neither ponder nor belabor such matters for a dear friend comes to our rescue, paying a visit armed with a gorgeous plant waiting to be potted. Not everything must be either decided or done on the spot; many empty "spaces" fill up of their accord. We must only be able to wait.

And thus I continue my tour to the newly planted bed of English roses. From afar it looks splendidly green and succulent. My spirits rise. But where on earth are the roses? Only upon closer inspection do I discover some yellowish and pink rose buds nestling amid opulent, plate-shaped nasturtiums. Hurrah! I had thought this type of rose bloomed only once! But whence all these nasturtiums? I can hardly resent their overgrowing everything: they are so incredibly beautiful with their water pearls set in the midst of their leaves. Of course, it occurs to me that there had been much rainfall during my absence, and now all last year's seeds have sprouted. In actual fact, they crowd out the roses, but why should they not not bide their time beside them? I am not a particularly tidy gardener; let surprises live, and look forward to the long tendrils growing rampant in autumn, spreading luminescent red, orange, and yellow flowers everywhere.

Moreover – the nasturtiums resist the snails, for which they deserve my praise.

I am also full of praise for my delightful blue Nigella damascena ("Love-in-a-mist"). These grow from every crack and corner, covering the ground with their blue stars that sit meditatively in the filigreed green. Their stamens are conglobate, almost like gooseberries, and are fun to observe when dried, too. They have an air of witchcraft and fairy tales. Something catches my eye in one part of the garden that renders me desperate rather than aggressive. I behold, or rather glimpse, the puny remains of my sunflowers. They are engulfed, entrapped, overgrown, and utterly covered in bindweed. Oh, what abject misery! Oh, good grief! Bindweed, the worst of all weeds!

Such a sight – together with the nearby forest edge advancing towards my garden (and hence calling for countermeasures), the blackberry tendrils inching their way into the lawn, the wisteria growing into the oblong flower boxes, and the Clematis montana threatening the roof – exhausts my thoughts and prompts me to declare in an fatigued voice: "Well, I suppose, I will have no choice either tomorrow or the day after!" Once again, the Latin phrase *Natura abhorret vacuum* ... (Nature abhors a vacuum) proves true: Nature grows rampant, and a garden remains a garden only if we set to work with hoe, rake, shears, and determination. To work! To work! To work!

Alicia Amherst's delightful little collection of gardeners' accounts of their labors offers some consolation in this respect, among many others the following wise words: "Perhaps the chiefest attraction of a garden is that occupation can always be found there. No idle people are happy, but with mind and fingers busy cares are soonest forgotten." (Alicia Amherst, 1902)[70]

Does this not reveal a profound truth, capable of reconciling us with our toil in the garden and yet which we take too little to heart? Namely, that working with our hands can have a relaxing and sobering effect on our soul or, phrased differently, that any labor occupying our mind and hands can render us content and happy.

Most of us know from personal experience that this is the case; in what follows, I wish to dwell more closely on why this holds true – to cast light on the positive aspects of gardening on the one hand, and to consider what working with our hands, which can be thoroughly creative, involves in general terms on the other.

Let me jog your memory for a moment: do you know a man who returns home frustrated and vexed after another day at the office, nags his family, and then – thank heavens – retires to the workroom? Once there, he sets to work, tinkering and cutting away, filing, and gluing together – all with his hands – some marvelous object – to later return to the dinner table purged and even-tempered. Or perhaps you know a man who relishes weeding the family garden with his bare hands, thus recovering from tiring, one-sided brain work? Have you ever experienced a sick child holing up in a corner to paint its fears or pain into a picture, thereby promoting its own healing? I have met women who can knead their pain or love into the dough of a cake they are baking or knit their delicate longing into a soft handmade pullover. Other women, among them myself, retreat to the garden armed with a hoe and pruning shears "to work with their hands" when their minds are troubled.

In the garden, something difficult to describe recurs, something that eludes reasoning: entrenched ideas and emotions begin to become unstuck, and consciousness loosens. Grievances are erased as if by a magic hand, and vague ideas assume new shape. It is as if immediate, sensual contact with the soil and plants has a soothing, softening effect on people. Their energies no longer circle around inner problems, but are drawn outward by nature's ever-surprising and fascinating vigor.

We behold an interestingly shaped leaf or a butterfly never seen before – one surprise entails another. Life energies begin to vibrate anew, and a positive, healing power spreads to our eyes, nose, and in particular our hands to affect our entire being. And – as Alicia Amherst observes – such beneficent "handwork" is amply available in the garden. Gardening thus constitutes a never-dwindling source of healing for our spiritual-mental and physical health! I utter these words with a faint smile, since I am well aware that many activities would be conducive to our health, were it not for convenience and comfort. But let us leave aside human laziness and other weaknesses to return to our hands, which never cease to exhaust our respect and love.

Our hands bridge the space between us and our surroundings; they connect the inner and outer world through rendering visible and tangible that inside us which seeks expression.[71] They deliver us, as it were, from our formative and creative urge. This urge is a profound human trait: we strive to, and must, actualize our inner life in the outer world. Much emotional suffering stems from blocked,

repressed impulses and ideas. Such unformed energies bloat us and induce suffering until we become active and shape these energies. Our principal tools for doing so are our hands. They literally "take things in hand," shaping the unshaped, thereby inducing a change that enables healing. It can thus happen that a person regains their balance through their hands. Gardening, as Alicia Amherst asserts, offers one possibility for self-healing.

Many other possibilities exist to become creative with our hands, among others tinkering and handicrafting, cooking, painting, writing, modeling, or playing with and shaping sand – which comes very close to gardening. Sandplay can involve either a children's sandbox or the sandtray I use in my work as a practising therapist, as mentioned at the outset.[72] Clients are given the possibility, through free, creative play, to set up a world corresponding to their inner state. We thus give our inner world a visible, three-dimensional form, which enables us to see and understand ourselves. We can give shape to happy, beautiful, and positive things; or we can render visible and comprehensible fears and burdensome memories in order to alter and resolve them. Our life energies flow anew, and new possibilities open up. Through caressing, kneading, and shaping the soil or sand, we are able to massage and reinvigorate our own blockages, hardenings, and stiffness.

Experience has taught me that such physical activity contributes significantly to influencing and healing the human soul and mind. The eminent anatomist Erich Blechschmidt describes these connections aptly in his book *Wie beginnt das menschliche Leben: vom Ei zum Embryo*.[73] In quoting a short passage, I am aware that it can hardly do justice to the book's overall significance: "When we marvel at the infant barely able to stand seeking to grasp everything around it, we realize that mental comprehension will not develop without physical touch. It takes time to grasp with the mind that which our hands can touch first. [...] Everyday language reveals how involved our hands are in sense-making. Thus, we speak of 'a *grasp* of the matter,' 'to be quick on the up*take*,' or 'to have pre*conceived* notions.' [...] Even the meaning of words like *hold* (an opinion), *take* (a view), *seize* (the day) is based on our body's prior somatic experience rather than perhaps mere logical reasoning. We are evidently able to develop an instrumental awareness when through the use of our hands we can appropriate for ourselves a way of thinking."[74]

Bodily activity thus precedes the formation of psychic structures and plays a decisive role in shaping these. Moreover, many of our bodily experiences occur very early in life and are highly individual and subjective – coupled with psychological imprints, emotions, and inner images that in most cases are buried in the unconscious.

These imprints, which are acquired in particular through our sense of touch, are later resurrected and reanimated through touch. Positive experiences can be appended to consciousness whereas negative ones can be balanced through new, positive imprints acquired, for example, through creativity learnt in a therapeutic setting. Since we associate sand or clay soil primarily with growth, fertility, life, and creative play, physical contact with it will have a healing and whole-making effect, not to mention working with it. Let me recall the small boy (see page 97) who rolled around on the warm spring soil, his entire body thus making contact with its positive force and growth!

I would like to cite another example of how making physical contact with soil and garden plants can contribute to healing the psyche. Our first and often crucial experience of body contact dates to infancy. Such contact, and the exchange it involves, can provide warmth, comfort, and reassurance. It helps infants gain confidence in their own bodies and their parents'. From early on, we learn that physical contact and touch can be a positive experience.

Other children experience such contact as either overbearing, stifling, and constraining, or indeed even as encroaching on their personal sphere and integrity. They are later inclined to avoid contact for fear of sensuous or intimate contact with others.

Experiencing too little contact, or none at all in the worst case, is just as serious as too much. Children deprived of body contact are prone to suffering later in life. They will withdraw into their own minds and shy away from approaching others in confidence. Quite often, they will suffer greatly and be prone to mistrust, fear, and sexual anxiety (the latter being associated with physical contact in adulthood).

This theme could obviously be developed in much greater depth, but this would alter the character of this book too much. Instead, I would rather recall Ginette Paris's observations about flowers, gardens, and Aphrodite (see Chapter 5): "Gardens express the sensuality of a culture, a type of sensuality that, for those whose educational background or age has caused them to ignore sexual vitality, offers the advantage of being without anxiety."[75]

Gardens thus provide a sheltered space in which physical, sensual contact with nature can be experienced fearlessly. Yet we still feel anxious, although neither the soil nor plants are evil, as noted. Quite on the contrary, they are generous and benevolent, affording shy and frightened individuals their beauty, moldability, and fertility, indeed their entire nature. Either a small or large garden offers the opportunity to engage in a circumspect manner with the physical world around us without violating it. The tenderness and body contact so very absent in childhood can be learned and accepted in the garden.

Do not small, affectionate flowers appear in our dreams because they wish to reveal and give us something? I realize that tender flowers are no substitute for affectionate and loving human beings, but the garden is nonetheless a world in-between, a point along the way in which we can experience and try out what was rendered impossible in early life and yet proves indispensable for fulfilled adulthood.

We can now once more return to the relationship between the soul of the garden and the garden of the soul. Given the connections between the inner and outer world described above, is it at all surprising how many threads we weave between the work undertaken in a garden and our inner life? Hardly, I would argue, since gardening is also a leisurely, contemplative activity affording us time to understand our feelings and opportunity for inner images. It is akin to knitting, embroidery, cooking, and baking, or writing letters (by hand). Such "female" activities proceed slowly, leaving time for reflection and – as mentioned – feeling.

True feeling, be it feeling for or empathizing with others or a course of events, or feeling our way into ourselves, needs time. Those who are guided by feeling are slow, for feeling ponders, wanders back and

forth, reaches outward to others, moves inward into the manifold layers of the soul, feels its way forward through light and shadow, through clarity and the nebulous; I recall the slow and steady process involved in weaving a carpet, through which a patterned image slowly emerges from the work of feeling (see page 19).

Even washing dishes can evoke inner images and feelings: a highly intelligent woman once told me that she relished dishwashing as it afforded her the opportunity for reflection or the time and leisure for those all-important, intimate conversations with her children. Likewise, harvesting berries, stringing beans, shelling peas, or weeding enhance emotional togetherness.

All such activities, or similar ones, proceed slowly and at a steady rhythm. We repeat the same movements for a certain time and as they become familiar our minds can drift and wander off. These tasks are hardly grandiose, nor intoxicating, but they have a soothing and balancing effect on our rather hectic lives and our overburdened cognitive and response apparatus.

Incidentally, these "female" chores are mostly associated with much love, such as lovingly preparing a meal for others or the kind thoughts that cross our mind when knitting a sweater or some warm baby socks. Drawing images in a picture book, planting tulips in a flowerpot, raking autumn leaves, or weeding can arouse such feelings, too.

Weeding is indeed the opposite of the motherly activity of planting seeds. We tear up, destroy, and throw away something hurtful or offensive. It even lends itself to releasing aggression. And it involves separating the wheat from the chaff, the useful or desirable from the unuseful or undesirable. It concerns establishing order, within and without.

But matters are somewhat complicated, for we all have different notions of an orderly garden, not to mention life. Some tear up every little herb and flower – even grass – that violates their personal sense of order. There is a perfectionism about these gardens, and they are quite uninteresting. Nothing unexpected or out of the ordinary blooms, and nature's pranks are reined in. Perhaps this explains why children dislike weeding, because they are prankish themselves, preferring to toy with the "wheat" and "chaff." Children, moreover, distinguish less between the "useful" and "unuseful," but rather between "like" and "dislike." They are not yet particularly suited to "serious" weeding.

Adults, however, can be deadly serious and sober weeders: they opt for a head of lettuce here and a tagetes there, or earmark this flower bed for white roses and another for small begonias. Which looks very neat and tidy, like a well-kept cemetery. The matter-of-fact weeder eliminates anything not resembling lettuce, tagetes, roses, or begonia. No overwintered seeds, for example nasturtium (do you recall my garden?), are allowed to grow, not a single poppy seed blown across the fence can flourish, and all incongruity will be eradicated. What kind of people might these be, I wonder? But I will leave you to consider this.

There is another, interesting approach to weeds. Ursula Buchan, for example, observes: "Weeds have a peculiar fascination for us. They are endlessly interesting, like an enemy who occupies our thoughts and schemes so much more than any friend and whom (though we would never admit it) we should miss if he suddenly moved away. I know the weeds in my garden better than most of my flowers and, without them, my victories would be insipid affairs. Weeds provide the challenge that most gardeners require. They may sometimes appear to us as ineradicable as Original Sin, but we would be sorry to have to admit that, like sin, we were not conscious of a strong urge to overcome them."[76]

This strikes me as a highly amusing insight into the business of weeds. Perhaps less so as far as actual weeds are concerned than our concept of the enemy we loathe so much, deplore incessantly, and yet cling to like leeches. Actual weeds are about as ineradicable as "original sin." But I cannot affirm the view that we cling to weeds or, if we do, then merely to celebrate victory in a war of annihilation. For occasionally we are seized with a wild, perhaps even violent urge to deal with buttercups, dandelions, bindweeds, and many more!

Buttercups and dandelions can be removed through applying patience and proper tools. Bindweeds, however, as we know, not only entangle all upward growth, but their roots burrow their way deep down in the ground only to reemerge where we least expect them. They become an inner burden, true and proper basket cases, comparable to chitchat and rumors! While they flower nicely (making fun of others is entertaining after all, and so is spreading talk or opinion or personal details or allegedly sensational news), gossip entraps and assaults personal freedom just as bindweeds attack our neighbor's plants. Their subterranean roots, moreover, spread maliciously like rumors only to reappear somewhere else to ensnare someone.

Bindweeds are also an apposite image for a secret craving for power. We assume we have wrenched it from our own souls, and conquered it. We endeavor to be good, restrain our claims to power, and, in particular, not to reveal them! Yet secretly they continue to crawl in the dark soil and our unconscious to emerge somewhere, sometime. Bindweeds of this kind are a most tedious weed in the soul garden, and eradicating them is a laborious affair. They run wild time and again. Should we perhaps cultivate rumors, claims to power, and bindweeds in a designated patch of soil or garden, since they are seemingly ineradicable and simply part of life?

We could invent a small garden in which to plant our most abominable "weeds," that is, our worst character traits, and surround these

with a towering wall. Obviously, the wall would need to reach far enough into the soil "because of the crawling bindweeds." We could place a couple of moralizers on the wall, armed with fine mesh butterfly nets, to catch all the flying seeds and trim the meddlesome, precocious bindweed with long shears.

On occasion, they would climb over the wall brandishing a sword to take on the weeds. After all, we want to celebrate victories and become heroes and heroines – in the battle against weeds! We will destroy them! Fortunately, weeds grow back quickly and forcefully, otherwise there would be no challenge for us to rise to in the garden, as our English gardener writes .... If only I had remembered this on my return from a splendid holiday when the sight of so much obnoxious growth infuriated me to the point of distraction! For then I would have turned into a heroine! Alas, all I did was break out into a routine sweat and groan, much like any other ordinary gardener. Everyday routine is simply that, neither more nor less, neither exciting nor depressing ....

I would like to return once more to plain gardening in the soul garden, about which there is nothing heroic. For nowadays, there are many people who experience their soul as an insignificant, barren garden. Others, including therapists, take a different view, but that seldom changes subjective perception for the better.

On the contrary, it almost appears as if those people's emotional ground refuses to become fruitful the more a therapist *consciously* endeavors to dig, water, and sow. The greater our effort to help and stimulate, the more these people appear to move away and close up. This causes therapists to seriously doubt their professional aptitude, and threatens their own soul gardens because the fruitless, tedious work in their patients' gardens exhausts their energy.

This predicament afflicted me until I realized that Leviticus's dictum could be rephrased thus: "Thou shalt love thy neighbor's soul garden as thine own." Or more broadly speaking: "Tidy your garden and ensure that your garden remains fertile and abloom, for this will please, inspire, and strengthen others." As therapists we are not obliged to plant our patient's garden. We neither promise nor plant them a garden of roses, but instead afford them a sheltered space in which they can grow their own. Besides, the wealth and strength of our spiritual world, our faith in both nature's healing powers and those of humankind, are transmitted silently to our patients and fellow beings, on invisible wings, as it were.

Just as the principle of resonance ensures that the vibrating strings of one musical instrument cause another to vibrate, the animated green within us quickens the desiccated "sacred force of greening" slumbering inside our patients. All at once, there is hope, as was the case with one of my patients. Following a long, difficult to bear, bleak period, in which neither a gleam of light shone nor a flower bloomed in her soul, this dream came to her:

> She discovered a small bag containing tulip bulbs among the books standing on my bookshelf. She took it secretly, carried it home, and planted the bulbs in her garden. She had the faint hope that the tulips would flower the following spring.

*

The dream awakened a sense of joy in my patient and sparked a glimmer of hope in me, too. Winter still loomed. It is a difficult season for many, for we no longer see what is happening "beneath the

149

soil," that is, in a person's deepest unconscious. Just as the legendary spring carpet had served Chosroes, the Sassanid king, as a faithful companion "recalling spring" (see pages 19 and 22), my patient's dream accompanied her over the next months. I fostered even the faintest sign of growth and alerted her to the fact that her contempt for the small, almost invisible stages of development forever sought to destroy the potential contained within her dream. I encouraged her to tread on the small leaves budding in her soul while expecting therapy to yield a magnificent harvest of blooms and fruit.

No matter how unspectacular it might sound, therapists are often like gardeners having to repeatedly instruct their patients that strong plants and tall trees have grown out of small seed leaves and require much time and care (and God's blessing) to develop; as mentioned, only those of us who have ever planted a garden will know what it comes down to. I trusted in the tulips, which she had planted in her dream, to bloom. And so they did, albeit very, very timidly, one after another, and we greeted their growth with delight.

It is time to return to the gnarled quince tree, my grandfather's favorite tree, which appeared to me in a dream many years ago (see Chapter 4). Almost fifty years have passed since my grandfather and I strolled through his garden, and almost twenty-five since the tree reappeared in my dream.

These were lengthy time periods in which the "quince tree," however, appeared within me in one shape or another. For example, I recall one of the countless images that shape and animate the soul, as described elsewhere in this book. It is *one* image from my life initially accompanied by very strong feelings of reverence and admiration for my grandfather, but which changed in manifold ways over time up to today where this beautiful and yet gnarled tree proves of great significance to how I see myself and my profession.

I dreamed that my grandparents' house was due to be demolished, and that I was assigned the task of saving my grandfather's quince tree and his collection of paintings done by the sick children in his care. He practised as a pediatrician and recognized early in his career that

his patients' drawings (paintings!) revealed a great deal about their spiritual and physical condition.

In the dream, I found myself in my grandparents' or rather in my grandfather's soul garden; that is, in a place suffused with his essence in which I, as a child, had also learned to observe nature, feel and love its soul, and intuitively perceive its spirit. Thus, I had been transported to this place to receive two important gifts: my grandfather's quince tree and his patients' drawings.

The quince tree belongs to the rosaceae or rose family (Aphrodite beckons!) and is native to western Asia. It is a splendidly beautiful, strong, gnarled, and expansive tree. Its blossoms recall apple blossoms, but their color is somewhat stronger. Ripe quinces are a resplendent golden yellow and combine the shape of an apple with a pear's. They were said to conjoin the male and female. In ancient Greece, they symbolized love and eros, and were given to the newly wed to bless their marriage with good fortune and consummation. Quinces also used to be highly esteemed in popular medicine. They served as a remedy against inflammations and – of particular interest with regard to my grandfather's occupation as a doctor – the quince tree protects those who are vulnerable on account of their sensitivity. The quince tree aids the suffering. Its fruits contain healing substances and symbolize love and relatedness. The entire tree strikes me as a marvelous symbol for medical and therapeutic occupations and hence deserves to be preserved within me.[77]

What about the sick children's images? As mentioned, the soul appears to be composed of countless inner images. These carry memories, feelings, thoughts, experiences, and visions. They form an amazingly rich world comprising all the ups and downs of life. Every image thus shows that a child or adult draws or paints part of their life and experience. Those who understand the pictorial language of the soul or the spiritual language of images will hear these images recount tales of joy, love, suffering, life, illness, and death.

The garden as a vessel for the quince tree protecting our anima and animus – we could thus weave this dream further – is *one* image that assumed shape in the outer garden, established itself and developed in the inner realm of my soul, and over time has become a strong general principle guiding my life. To become aware of this principle, I had to push open the heavy, Oriental gate in the dream I recounted at the beginning of this book, and go for long walks in the garden stretching out behind it. This connection became plainly evident to me while walking, pausing, contemplating, and feeling my way forward. Much remains partially concealed, however, since it is the nature of gardens to lead us back and forth, here and there, onto heights and into depths. After a time, we believe we know them; and yet – they disallow being fully known. They soon cast a new veil over their secrets, leaving us to marvel and question, and be captured anew by their magic.

Acknowledgments

For their generous support for the English translation of my book, I would like to express my deepest gratitude to Robert and Maria Kelly. Their contributions through Guardian Stewardship encourage the study and experience of the depth dimension in the psyche, particularly Carl Jung's discoveries, including the symbolic meanings of House and Garden.

I would also like to thank Mark Kyburz and John Peck for their excellent translation from German, and Robert Hinshaw and his staff at the Daimon Verlag for publishing my garden book.

Ruth Ammann

Notes

1 Merlin and Vivian are among the figures in King Arthur's legends. Both are still very much alive in Brittany, in particular in its "heart," Brocéliande's magic forest. Here, the visitor discovers "Merlin's grave," "Vivian's grave," "Vivian's castle," and other enchanted places. Possibly, however, Merlin lived far earlier; on this, see Tolstoy, Nikolai: *The Quest for Merlin*. Sceptre, Sevenoaks 1988.

2 On the subject of "otherworlds," see, for instance, Hetmann, Frederik: *Die Reise in die Anderswelt*. Diederichs, Munich 1981.

3 During World War Two, the lawns of private gardens were used to grow potatoes and vegetables. In common parlance, this was the "scramble to grow crops [*Anbauschlacht*]."

4 On the imagination, see Jung, Carl Gustav: *Gesammelte Werke*, Vol. 12, p. 317 ff. Walter, Zurich 1972.

5 Ford, P.R.J.: *Oriental Carpet Design: A Guide to Traditional Motifs, Patterns and Symbols*. Thames and Hudson, London 1981, p. 144.

6 Gothein, Marie Luise: *Geschichte der Gartenkunst*, Vol.1. Diederichs, München (Jena) 1926, p. 148 f.

7 Margulis, Lynn/Sagon, Dorion: *What is Life?* Simon & Schuster, New York 1995, p. 26.

8 On alchemy, see Jung, Carl Gustav: *Gesammelte Werke*, op.cit.

9 On fence riders, see Dürr, Hans Peter: *Traumzeit*. Syndikat, Frankfurt/M. 1983.

10 See any standard edition of *Grimm's Fairy Tales*.

11 On boundary sacrifices, see Sträuble, Bechtold: *Handwörterbuch des Deutschen Aberglaubens*. de Gruyter, Berlin/Leipzig 1931, especially the section entitled "Grenze," p. 1137.

12 Ammann, Ruth: *Traumbild Haus*. Walter, Zurich 1987.

13 Jung, Carl Gustav: *Memories, Dreams, Reflections*. Recorded & ed. Aniela Jaffé, tr. Richard & Clara Winston. Pantheon, New York 1963, p. 359.

14 The scale model of medieval Cluny is on exhibition at the Musée Ochier, Cluny.

15 The Château de Vaux le Vicomte is located southeast of Paris.

16 The Château de Villandry is situated near Tours in central France.

17 Jung, Garl Gustav: *Memories, Dreams, Reflections*. op.cit., p. 160.

18 The Bible. Authorized King James Version – my emphases.

19 Schimmel, Annemarie: Gärten der Erkenntnis. Das Buch der vierzig Sufi-Meister. Diederichs, München und Besserman, Perle: Der versteckte Garten. Die Kabbala als Quelle spiritueller Unterweisung. Fischer, Frankfurt/M. 1996.

20 Bredekamp, Horst: Botticelli Primavera. Fischer Tb, Frankfurt/M. 1988

21 Busch, Wilhelm: Gesamtausgabe, Vol. 2: "Die fromme Helene." Braun und Schneider, Munich 1943.

22 Ammann, Ruth: Heilende Bilder der Seele. Das Sandspiel – der schöpferische Weg der Persönlichkeitsentwicklung. Kösel, München 1989.

23 On tortoises, see, for instance, Heinz-Mohr, Gerd: Lexikon der Symbole, Diederichs, Munich 1983.

24 See the catalogue of the Gemäldegalerie Berlin, Berlin-Dahlem 1975.

25 Ibid.

26 Ibid.

27 Grimm's Fairy Tales, no. 76 "The Carnation."

28 On Selene, see Gottschalk, Herbert: Lexikon der Mythologie. Safari, Berlin 1973.

29 Paris, Ginette: Pagan Meditations: The Worlds of Aphrodite, Artemis, and Hestis. Spring Publications, Woodstock, Connecticut 1986, pp. 19-20.

30 Ibid., p. 20.

31 On Hecate, see Gottschalk, Herbert: Lexikon der Mythologie, op.cit.

32 Polunin, Miriam/Robbins, Christopher: The Natural Pharmacy, Dorling Kindersley, London 1992.

33 Gallwitz, Esther: Kleiner Kräutergarten. Insel, Frankfurt/M./Leipzig 1992; see especially the chapter entitled "Pflanzenkörper, Pflanzenseele," p. 22 f.

34 Polunin, M./Robbins, Ch.: The Natural Pharmacy, op.cit.

35 Golowin, Sergius: Die Magie der verbotenen Märchen. Merlin, Hamburg 1995.

36 Italienische Märchen, Märchen der Weltliteratur. Diederichs, München 1959, "Petrosinella"; Calvino, Italo: Fiabe italiane. Vol. I, Mondadori 1968, "Prezzemolina."

37 von Franz, Marie-Louise: Traum und Tod. Kösel, München 1984, p. 56. On Dreams and Death; A Jungian Interpretation, trs. Emmanuel Kennedy and Vernon Brooks, Shambhala, Boston & London 1986, p. 31.

38 Hepper, F. Nigel: Pharaoh's Flowers. London HMSO 1990, p. 54.

39 Handbuch der Religionsgeschichte, Vol. I. Vandenhoeck und Ruprecht, Göttingen 1971.

40 Ibid.

41 Endres, Franz Carl: *Mystik und Magie der Zahlen.* Rascher, Zurich 1951, p. 135

42 Paris, Ginette: *Pagan Meditations*, p. 20.

43 Ibid., p. 23 ff.

44 In our family, we use blackberry juice, sugar, and cornstarch to make this particular jelly. It ought to be thickish and "garnished" with liquid cream.

45 Polunin, M./Robbins, Ch.: *The Natural Pharmacy*, op.cit.

46 Scherf, Walter: *Lexikon der Zaubermärchen.* Kröner, Stuttgart 1982, p. 306

47 Calvino, Italo: *Fiabe italiane.* Vol. 2, "Rosmarina," op.cit.

48 von Kamphoevener, Elsa S.: *An Nachtfeuern der Karawan-Serail*, Vol. 2. "Das Bazilikonmädchen," Ex Libris, Frankfurt/M. (Zürich) 1977

49 Pesto is an Italian sauce, consisting largely of finely ground basil leaves, mixed with pasta.

50 Boccaccio, Giovanni: *Decameron*, Fourth Day, Fifth Novella. Trans. Guido Waldman. Oxford University Press: Oxford & New York 1998.

51 Ibid.

52 Barz, Ellynor: *Götter und Planeten.* Kreuz, Stuttgart 1988, p. 78 ff.

53 *Erzählungen aus den Tausendundein Nächten.* Insel, Frankfurt/M. 1953

54 Bassani, Giorgio: *The Garden of the Finzi-Continis.* Trans. William Weaver. Everyman's Library: New York 2005.

55 Hodgson Burnett, Frances: *The Secret Garden.* Bantam, New York 1987.

56 Ammann, Ruth: *Traumbild Haus*, op.cit.

57 Very decorative dream catchers are on sale in Native American shops in Northwestern America.

58 Hennebo, Dieter: *Gärten des Mittelalters.* Artemis, Zurich/Dusseldorf 1987; see especially the chapter entitled "Erotik in der Gartenkunst," p. 51 ff.

59 Schulze Peter H.: *Frauen im alten Ägypten.* Lübbe, Bergisch-Gladbach 1987, p. 39.

60 The chapel in question is the Royal Chapel in Windsor Park outside London. I am referring to Mary, Queen Mother of Great Britain and Ireland (1867-1953).

61 Swimme, Brian: *The Universe is a Green Dragon: A Cosmic Creation Story.* Bear and Company 1984. Cited here from the online version available at www.context.org/ICLIB/IC12/Swimme.htm (accessed on 24 January 2008).

62 Ibid.

63 Riedel, Ingrid: *Hildegard von Bingen. Prophetin der kosmischen Weisheit.* Kreuz, Stuttgart 1994.

64 Ibid., p. 11 ff.

65 Swimme, Brian: *op.cit*

66 On dragon symbolism, see Huxley, Francis: *The Dragon – nature of spirit, spirit of nature*. Thames and Hudson, London 1979.

67 Margulis Lynn/Sagon, Dorion: *What is Life?*

68 Autopoiesis, from Gree, literally means "auto (self)-creation," and denotes the continuous self-organization of life.

69 Margulis, Lynn/Sagon, Dorion: *What is Life?*, p. 175.

70 Kellaway, Deborah: *Women Gardeners*. Virago Press, London 1996

71 Ammann, Ruth: *Heilende Bilder der Seele*, op.cit.

72 Ibid.

73 Blechschmidt, Erich: *Wie beginnt das menschliche Leben: vom Ei zum Embryo. Forschungsergebnisse mit weitreichenden Folgen*. Stein a. Rhein 1989, p. 149 ff.

74 Ibid.

75 Paris, Ginette: *Pagan Meditations*, p. 20.

76 Kellaway, Deborah: *Women Gardeners*, p. 7.

77 On the quince and the quince tree, see Strassmann, Rene A.: *Baumheilkunde*, AT Verlag, Aarau 1994, p. 211.

Suggested Further Reading

Bianca, Stefano: *Hofhaus und Paradiesgarten. Architektur und Lebensformen in der islamischen Welt.* C.H. Beck, München 1991

Caroll-Spillecke, M.: *Der Garten von der Antike bis zum Mittelalter.* Zabern, Mainz 1995

Hauser, Albert: *Bauern-Gärten der Schweiz.* Artemis, Zürich/Düsseldorf 1976

Sackville-West, Virginia: *The Illustrated Garden Book.* Mermaid Books (Penguin Books), London 1989

Schultes, Richard E./Hofmann, Albert: *Pflanzen der Götter. Die magischen Kräfte der Rausch- und Giftgewächse.* AT Verlag, Aarau 1995

Stammel, Heinz J.: *Die Apotheke Manitous. Das medizinische Wissen der Indianer und ihre Heilpflanzen.* Rowohlt, Reinbek b. Hbg. 1986

Teichert, Wolfgang: *Gärten – Paradiesische Kulturen.* Kreuz, Stuttgart 1986

Vessichelli Pane, Rita: *Il Giardino.* Edizioni Olivares, Mailand 1994

Sources of Illustrations

From the author's private archive: pages 9 (Roses, watercolor, R.A.); 13 (Villa Medicea in Careggi, Florence); 15 (private garden, England); 16 (Alhambra, Granada/Spain); 17 (Alcazar, Sevilla/Spain); 18 (private garden); 20/21 (garden in Ireland); 26 (woodcut from Vadian's "Hortulus," 1512 edition. Source: Albert Hauser, Bauerngärten der Schweiz, Artemis); 27 (Marrakesh/Morocco); 28 (private garden); 32 (early sixteenth-century woodcut. Source: Dieter Fennebo, Gärten des Mittelalters, Artemis); 34 (my garden goblin); 36 (private garden, central London); 39 (private garden); 42 above (private house); 42 below (scale model of medieval Cluny/France); 43 (front garden, London); 44 (Garden, Château Vaux le Vicomte/France); 45 (Garden, Château de Villandry, Loire/France); 46/47 (The Savill Garden near Windsor/England); 49 (Villa Garzoni, Collodi near Pescia/Italy); 51 (Sissinghurst, Kent/England); 55 above ("Statue of Apennin," Villa Pratolino, Florence); 55 below (Fountain, Alcazar Gardens, Sevilla/Spain); 56 (Garden of the Maison de Claude Monet in Giverny/France); 65 (vegetable stall with "male" vegetables); 70 (The Savill Garden near Windsor/England); 73 (Jan van Eyck, "Portrait of a Man with Carnation"); 75 (private garden, Zurich); 77 (vegetable stall with "female" fruit); 83 (Hathor Temple, Dendera/Egypt); 104 (moon landscape, watercolor, R.A.); 108 (water lily pond in the garden at the Maison de Claude Monet, Giverny/France); 110 (The Savill Garden near Windsor/England); 113 (Generaliffe Garden, Alhambra, Granada/Spain); 122/123 (Windsor Park, England); 124 (Catholic Mission, Carmel / West Coast USA); 131 (Garden, Villa Gamberaia, Florence); 139 ("Green Fairy," London); 140 (Hands in sandtray, from: Ruth Ammann, *Heilende Bilder der Seele*); 143 ("Gärtchen," Small Garden, Kloster Ittingen/Switzerland);
Page 61 (Sandro Botticelli, "La Primavera," Galleria degli Uffizi, Florence)
Page 128 ("Annunciation of the Blessed Virgin Mary." Sacramentary from Cologne, 1000 A.D. Paris, National Library. Kunstverlag Maria Laach Nr. 5548)
All other pictures are from the author's collection.

Susan Bach

Life paints its own Span

The pioneering work, Life Paints Its Own Span, with over 200 color reproductions, is a comprehensive exposition of Susan Bach's original approach to the physical and psychospiritual evaluation of spontaneous paintings and drawings by severely ill patients. At the same time, this work is a moving record of Susan Bach's own journey of discovery.

Part I (Text): 208 pages
Part II (Pictures): 56 pages
ISBN 978-3-85630-516-1

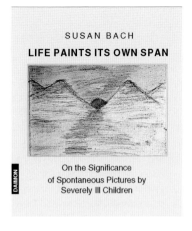

SUSAN BACH

LIFE PAINTS ITS OWN SPAN

On the Significance
of Spontaneous Pictures by
Severely Ill Children

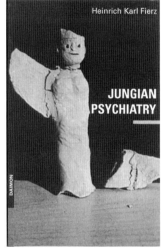

Heinrich Karl Fierz

Jungian Psychiatry

C.G. Jung spent the first ten years of his career working in a psychiatric clinic, an experience which had a powerful influence on his lifelong endeavors. Now the psychiatric-analytic observations of a highly respected Jungian, the Swiss Heinrich Fierz, who devoted his life to psychiatry, are available in English at last. Jungian Psychiatry is rich with the insights of a rare therapist and teacher in the world of the psychiatric clinic.

Heinrich Karl Fierz worked as a psychiatrist at the famed Binswanger Clinic, Sanatorium Bellevue, for many years before co-founding the Jungian "Klinik am Zürichberg" in 1964, where he was medical director until his recent death. A son of one of the first Jungian analysts, Linda Fierz-David, he also became a training analyst and lecturer at the Jung Institute in Zürich. His sensitive and innovative contributions to the realm of psychiatry are well-known in the German-speaking world; »Jungian Psychiatry« is the first major publication of his work in English.

420 pages, numerous illustrations, ISBN 978-3-85630-521-5

Sandplay Therapy
Treatment of Psychopathologies
Edited by Eva Pattis Zoja

Sandplay Therapy
Treatment of Psychopathologies

Ten European sandplay therapists describe how severe psychopathologies can be treated in the 'free and protected space' of the sandbox.

The sandplay therapy cases in this book illustrate some of the most difficult, yet also most effective applications: psychoses, borderline syndromes, psychosomatic illnesses, drug addictions, or narcissistic character disorders.

Ruth Ammann
Lorenzo Bignamini
Wilma Bosio
Franco Castellana
Vito La Spina
Stefano Marinucci
Marcella Merlino
Francesco Montecchi
Andreina Navone
Eva Pattis Zoja

Edited by Eva Pattis Zoja

DAIMON

Sandplay seems to access areas of human suffering which have otherwise always resisted psychotherapeutic treatment.

Recent research in neuroscience explains why this is possible: trauma is not remembered in verbal form – what has never been articulated in words nor ever 'shaped' cannot be outwardly expressed. In sandplay, however, 'it' manifests itself as a form, shaped by the hands.

The inexpressible can be seen and touched – therefore, it can be transformed.

272 pages, illustrated, ISBN 978-3-85630-622-9

A Testament to the Wilderness
Ten Essays on an Address by C.A. Meier

Daimon Verlag   The Lapis Press

C.A. Meier

A Testament to the Wilderness

In 1983, Swiss psychiatrist C.A. Meier delivered a fascinating paper at the 3rd World Wilderness Congress in Inverness, Scotland. "Wilderness and the Search for the Soul of Modern Man" addressed not only the tragedy of our vanishing natural wilderness and the need to preserve it, but also the necessity of preserving man's 'inner wilderness.' A Testament to the Wilderness consists of Meier's original address and thoughtful and provocative responses by nine concerned writers from around the world. (Laurens van der Post, Henderson, Wheelwright ...)

142 pages,
hardcover ISBN 978-3-85630-502-4, paperback ISBN 978-3-85630-503-1

ENGLISH TITLES FROM DAIMON